LAW OF THE LAND

A Practical Legal Guide for Tourists and Business Travelers

Turkey

By Michael L. Moore Esq.

Author: Michael L. Moore

Edited by Ally Knez-Siddique

Cover Design: Kristina Conatser

Published by: Law of the Land Publishing, LLC

ISBN: 978-1-964870-23-6

DEDICATION

This book is dedicated to the memory of my late older brother, Kenneth Lee Moore, whose tragic murder at 15 years of age inspired me to write this series of books.

This book is also dedicated to my parents, John Henry Moore, and Edna Mae Moore, whose tremendous parenting skills kept me focused on the important things in life: being reverent, getting educated, and prioritizing family.

Finally, this book is dedicated to my beautiful family, my wife, my son, and my daughter. They inspire me every single day to be kind, patient, and compassionate.

IN LOVING MEMORY OF:

Belinda Joyce Moore Moss—my beautiful and wonderful sister, who supported me in every positive thing that I ever attempted to do.

Michael Eugene Baker—my dedicated and loyal friend and brother, who always wanted the very best for me.

Sylvia Joyce Hill—my eldest sister, who had a beautiful spirit and was like a second mother to me.

PREFACE

My introduction to the justice system came when I was only 10 years old. My 15-year-old brother was murdered with a butcher knife by a 19-year-old in a simple argument over a torn shirt. I was devastated by his death and sought retribution for his fate that never came. The woman was initially charged with second degree murder, but after plea negotiations, she was convicted of manslaughter and sentenced to only five years in a youthful offender school and ordered to undergo psychiatric care. That was it. Nothing more. The judicial system had run its course.

My family knew nothing about the justice system, and we did not have the tools to advocate for ourselves. No one provided us with a written source to reference for guidance through this process. There was no easily accessible, easy to understand, definitive source to educate ourselves about the legal system that we suddenly and unexpectedly found ourselves immersed in after being victimized by such a violent criminal act.

As I got older, finished college, law school, and ultimately started practicing law, it became clear to me that most people are not knowledgeable about the law or how the judicial process works. If most people are uninformed here in the United States regarding the law and the legal process, how would they fare when in other countries? I realized that tourists and businesspeople who travel internationally needed access to information on how to navigate the legal system in other countries!

For many years, there has been considerable media attention focused on international travelers experiencing legal difficulties while traveling abroad. Most of these news stories gained attention in the United States and abroad because they involved American citizens facing punishment that was considered "unconventional" and "harsh" by United States' legal standards. I recall a news story in 1994 regarding Michael Fay, a young American male, who had broken the law in Singapore. He was convicted and sentenced to be caned and or whipped publicly. While the United States Government weighed in on the inappropriate and cruel nature of the punishment, the young American was beaten because he had been convicted under Singapore law.

Similarly, in recent years, international news stories have garnered headlines regarding foreign travelers and their issues with the laws of countries that were not their own. Amanda Knox, an American woman, was accused of murdering her roommate in Italy in 2007 and spent almost four years in an Italian prison before being definitively acquitted by the Supreme Court of Cassatio. Kenneth Bae, an American citizen, was arrested in North Korea in 2012 and was convicted for hostile acts against the communist country. He was sentenced to 15 years hard labor but was released in 2014 after efforts by the U.S. State Department. More recently, United States Basketball Star, Brittany Griner was arrested in February 2022 at a Moscow airport on drug-related charges and detained for nearly 10 months, spending much of that time in prison. Her plight unfolded at the same time Russia invaded Ukraine and further heightened tensions between Russia and the United States, ending only after she was freed in exchange for a notorious Russian arms dealer.

It was in 1994 that another personal tragic event occurred that finally inspired me to write these series of books. A dear friend and also client of mine was brutally murdered while on his second honeymoon in Jamaica. News of his murder shocked me and our local community. The legal hurdles his family had to overcome to see that justice was properly dispensed far away from home, in another country, with an entirely different set of criminal procedural rules and laws, was difficult to navigate.

As I was my friend's attorney at the time of his death, his family asked that I act as their "legal liaison" to the Jamaican Prosecutor's Office and to the Jamaican Police Department. I participated in multiple police interviews with my client's widow because she was the primary witness to his murder. As a former prosecuting attorney, I was also allowed by the Court, as a professional courtesy, to sit at the prosecutor's table to consult with the prosecuting attorney during trial. What I observed about the Jamaican trial process from a front row seat was compelling enough to cause me to seriously consider educating the "world" regarding what to expect and how to act appropriately when faced with legal issues while traveling abroad.

One of the realities in life is that, regardless of what country you are in, it is never a pleasant experience to run afoul of the law and be forced to accept that someone else will be making a decision about your pecuniary, proprietary, or penal interests (your money, your property, or your freedom).

It is important to know what the laws are, how they apply to you, and how to navigate the legal system if you are charged with a crime. It is also very helpful to know what resources are available to you if you are the victim of a criminal act. At the end of the day, an "ounce of prevention is worth a pound of cure," so the more knowledge you have, the more ammunition you possess, and the more likely you will have a positive outcome.

If you are traveling to Turkey, the first thing you should pack is a copy of this book! The helpful information and tips contained in this volume will provide a great starting point for knowing what to do (and not to do!) when you arrive at your destination and will help ensure that you have a wonderful vacation or business trip unmarred by tangles with the law.

TABLE OF CONTENTS

INTRODUCTION

IN THIS CHAPTER

- About This Book
- Hypotheticals Used Throughout This Book
- How This Book is Organized
- Icons Used in This Book
- Where to Go From Here

INTRODUCTION

As a practicing attorney for over 34 years, I have encountered numerous clients who travel often, but are unaware of the laws of the land they are traveling to.

Therefore, many years ago, I decided to write a series of books that would explain the laws of specific countries. My focus was to explain the laws that may affect travelers in a straightforward manner, without all of the legal language that is sometimes hard for even seasoned attorneys to understand.

About This Book

The aim of this book is simple. It provides you, the traveler, with a simple, easy to read book that will provide a basic legal guide that explains the law in the country that you are about to visit. It is not intended to educate you on ALL of the laws in a given country. The goal is to provide you with the details of the most common legal and safety issues faced by tourists and business travelers.

I have also provided context with background information on places not to visit, statistics on the country and prevention measures you should take to safeguard your legal and physical safety. Knowledge is a powerful thing and knowing how to stay out of trouble (or how to get out of it!) is important for everyone who travels.

This *Law of The Land/Turkey* book simply helps you become more informed about your legal rights, responsibilities, and obligations in a wide range of subject areas.

Last, but not least, this book does NOT purport to offer legal advice. It does, however, provide the information you need to stay safe, follow the law and navigate around legal difficulties. However, if you do face legal difficulties, the information in this book will provide you with a starting point for solving the problem and obtaining legal assistance should it be required.

Hypotheticals Used Throughout This Book

From time to time throughout this book, I will explain the law to readers by using hypothetical scenarios. These hypotheticals will be marked by an icon that will be explained in further detail as you read on.

How This Book is Organized

CHAPTER 1: **About Turkey.** This chapter will provide you with a brief overview about Turkey and its history. It also addresses Visa requirements, monetary advice, and the best times to visit.

CHAPTER 2: **Customs.** This chapter will provide information on what to expect when entering Turkey. It will also explain what restricted and prohibited items are when entering Turkey along with custom's regulations.

CHAPTER 3: **Crime in Turkey.** This chapter provides an overview of the history of crime in Turkey and steps that Turkish officials have taken to curb the high rate of crime.

CHAPTER 4: **Criminal Law Violations.** This chapter will provide information on drug offenses, penalties, true events and questions and answers.

CHAPTER 5: **Alcohol-Related Offenses.** This chapter will provide key points regarding the sale, consumption, and regulations of alcohol use in Turkey.

CHAPTER 6: **Firearm & Ammunition Offenses.** This chapter will provide key points regarding the possession of firearms and ammunition in Turkey.

CHAPTER 7: **Prostitution.** This chapter provides an overview of the history of prostitution in Turkey, laws and penalties, prostitution practices, sex trafficking, sex tourism, health in Turkey, tips to avoid being hassled, a Law of the Land Hypothetical, and the current situation on prostitution in Turkey.

CHAPTER 8: **LGBTQ.** This chapter will provide information regarding the acceptance of LGBTQ people in Turkey and the laws surrounding homosexuality.

CHAPTER 9: **Sexually Motivated/Violent Crimes.** This chapter will provide an overview of sexually related crimes in Turkey.

CHAPTER 10: **Arrested in Turkey.** This chapter will provide information on what to do if you are arrested in Turkey.

CHAPTER 11: **Jails vs. Prisons: Conditions & Culture.** This chapter will provide information on the conditions and culture of Turkish Jails and Prisons.

CHAPTER 12: **Helping a Friend or Relative Imprisoned in Turkey.** This chapter will provide information on how you can assist a friend or relative imprisoned in Turkey.

CHAPTER 13: **The Administration of Justice.** This chapter will provide information on Turkey's Legal System.

CHAPTER 14: **Crime Victim Assistance.** This chapter will provide information on crime victim assistance along with providing safety tips.

CHAPTER 15: **Police.** This chapter will provide information on the Turkish Police and how to report a crime.

CHAPTER 16: **How to Get Legal Help in Turkey.** This chapter will provide information regarding how to obtain legal assistance for travelers to Turkey.

CHAPTER 17: **Medical Facilities & Hospitals.** This chapter will provide information about how to obtain medical care while visiting Turkey.

CHAPTER 18: **Driving in Turkey.** This chapter will provide information on driving in Turkey, it's traffic rules, and road safety tips.

CHAPTER 19: **Nude Beaches & Clothing-Optional Resorts.** This chapter will provide an overview of nude beaches and clothing-optional resorts in Turkey, and the legality and safety of visiting nude beaches in Turkey.

CHAPTER 20: **Unusual Laws.** This chapter will provide information on some Unusual Laws in Turkey, and penalties and fines.

CHAPTER 21: **Traveling Safely.** This chapter will provide information on women traveling alone, crime prevention for families, safety notes for all travelers, and overall advice.

CHAPTER 22: **Tourist Taxation.** This chapter will provide information on taxes that tourists are required to pay in Turkey.

CHAPTER 23: **Long-Term Stays.** This chapter will provide an overview of the consequences for overstaying your visit to Turkey.

CHAPTER 24: **Civil Litigation.** This chapter will provide information about the civil litigation process in Turkey.

CHAPTER 25: **Other Things to Know.** This chapter will provide information on the harassment of tourists, travel and safety, and other practical tips.

CHAPTER 26: **Quick Reference Guide.** This chapter is a quick way to get information. It is a condensed version of the chapters in this book.

Emergency/Important Contact Numbers in Turkey

Useful Turkish Phrases

Glossary

Icons Used in this Book

What do those pictures throughout the book mean? See below:

WARNING: This icon flags information about things you should **avoid** while visiting Turkey. Heed the advice next to this icon to avoid legal perils.

REMEMBER: This icon flags noteworthy information that you **shouldn't forget.**

HELPFUL TIPS: This icon flags information that will help you when entering Turkey, relates to a legal situation, or refers to resources available while visiting Turkey.

TECHNICAL INFORMATION: This icon flags technical aspects of the law. If you are faced with a legal problem, and you want to learn more about the law involved, this information can be helpful.

ADDITIONAL INFORMATION: This icon points to the location of additional information available on the internet.

HYPOTHETICAL: This icon points to hypothetical scenarios to illustrate possible legal problems and the outcome.

QUESTIONS: This icon points to questions and answers throughout the book.

TRUE STORY: This icon points to true events throughout the book.

Where to Go From Here

If you have a specific question about the law in Turkey as it relates to a particular area, just turn to the chapter that addresses that issue, or turn to the Quick Reference Guide. You can also read the book from cover to cover to obtain a more comprehensive understanding of Turkish laws and resources available should you find yourself in a legal predicament while visiting.

Disclaimer: While the recommendations in this book primarily address U.S. citizens, the information is relevant and applicable to citizens of any country.

CHAPTER 1

ABOUT TURKEY

IN THIS CHAPTER

- About Turkey
- Turkey, the Basics
- Turkish Hospitality

CHAPTER 1
ABOUT TURKEY

About Turkey

Turkey is a transcontinental country located mainly on the Anatolian Peninsula in Western Asia, with a smaller portion on the Balkan Peninsula in Southeastern Europe. It is bordered by eight countries: Greece and Bulgaria to the northwest; Georgia to the northeast; Armenia, Azerbaijan, and Iran to the east; and Iraq and Syria to the south. The country is surrounded by the Mediterranean Sea to the south, the Aegean Sea to the west, and the Black Sea to the north. It also controls the Bosporus, the Sea of Marmara, and the Dardanelles—strategic waterways linking Europe and Asia. Covering an area of **about 783,562 square kilometers (302,535 square miles)**, Turkey is larger than any European Union country in terms of land area. As of 2025, it has a population of **roughly 86 million people**, making it one of the most populous countries in its region.

Turkey is well known for its rich blend of Eastern and Western cultures, dramatic landscapes, and deep historical heritage. Visitors are drawn to its diverse scenery—from Mediterranean beaches and Cappadocia's fairy chimneys to the mountains of Eastern Anatolia. Turkey's cuisine, famous for dishes like kebabs, baklava, meze, and Turkish tea, is a flavorful mix of Middle Eastern, Central Asian, Balkan, and Mediterranean influences. The country is also renowned for its bustling bazaars, Ottoman architecture, and ancient ruins, including Ephesus, Troy, and Göbekli Tepe—the world's oldest known temple complex. Istanbul, its largest city, uniquely straddles two continents, offering a living bridge between Europe and Asia.

Short History

The land that is now Turkey has been home to countless civilizations, including the **Hittites, Phrygians, Greeks, Romans,** and **Byzantines**. It later became the heart of the powerful **Ottoman Empire**, which lasted from the late 13th century until its dissolution after World War I. In 1923, the Republic of Turkey was founded by **Mustafa Kemal Atatürk**, who implemented sweeping reforms to modernize the country, secularize its government, and promote national unity. Throughout the 20th and 21st centuries, Turkey has experienced political, social, and economic transformations, balancing its identity between its Islamic heritage and secular governance, as well as between European and Middle Eastern influences.

The Capital

Ankara, located in central Anatolia, is Turkey's capital and **second-largest city.** Chosen by Atatürk for its strategic location and symbolism of a fresh start, Ankara serves as the nation's political and administrative hub. While less visited than Istanbul, Ankara offers cultural attractions like the Museum of Anatolian Civilizations, Atatürk's Mausoleum (Anıtkabir), and vibrant districts filled with cafes, markets, and universities.

The People

The people of Turkey, known as **Turks,** are ethnically diverse, with **Kurdish, Arab, Circassian, Laz,** and **other minority communities** adding to the cultural mosaic. Family ties are strong, hospitality is highly valued, and guests are often offered tea or coffee as a gesture of warmth. While urban centers are fast-paced and cosmopolitan, rural areas tend to preserve more traditional lifestyles and customs. Turkish society blends modern influences with deep-rooted traditions, resulting in a unique national character.

Language

The official language is **Turkish,** written in the Latin alphabet since Atatürk's reforms in 1928. **Kurdish** (mainly Kurmanji dialect) is also widely spoken in the southeast, along with other minority languages. **English** is increasingly taught in schools and is commonly used in tourist areas, but proficiency levels vary outside major cities.

Religion

Turkey is officially a secular state, but the majority of its population—about 99%—is **Muslim**, predominantly Sunni, with a significant Alevi minority. There are also small **Christian** and **Jewish** communities. Religious practices vary widely; in urban areas, many people lead secular lifestyles, while in rural regions, traditions may be more conservative. Religious festivals, such as Ramadan and Eid al-Adha, are important cultural occasions, often celebrated with family gatherings and shared meals.

Affordability

Turkey is generally considered **affordable** compared to Western Europe. The cost of living and travel expenses are lower, especially outside major tourist hubs. In Istanbul or coastal resorts, prices can be higher but still offer good value for money. A night in a mid-range hotel might cost between ₺1,200–₺2,000 ($40–$65 USD), while budget options can be found for much less. Meals at local restaurants typically range from ₺150–₺300 ($5–$10 USD), and street food like simit or dürüm is even cheaper. Public transportation is inexpensive, with metro or bus fares around ₺15–₺25 ($0.50–$0.85 USD). Long-distance buses and domestic flights are also cost-effective for traveling between regions. Many historic sites have modest entry fees, and outdoor attractions like beaches, markets, and natural parks are often free to enjoy.

Turkey, the Basics

How to Get There?

Turkey is a major travel hub linking Europe, Asia, and the Middle East, making it one of the most accessible destinations in its region. It is well-connected by air to cities across North America, Europe, Asia, Africa, and the Middle East. With multiple international airports handling millions of passengers each year, Turkey offers a wide range of travel options—from full-service international carriers to budget-friendly regional airlines.

Major airports in Turkey include:

- **Istanbul Airport** (**IST**) – Opened in 2018 on the European side of Istanbul, IST is now one of the largest airports in the world and Turkey's main international gateway. It handles flights from over 350 destinations worldwide and is the primary hub for Turkish Airlines, which offers extensive connections across Europe, Asia, Africa, and the Americas.
- **Sabiha Gökçen International Airport** (**SAW**) – Located on the Asian side of Istanbul, SAW is the city's second major airport and a hub for low-cost carriers such as Pegasus Airlines. It serves numerous European and Middle Eastern destinations and is popular with budget-conscious travelers.
- **Ankara Esenboğa Airport** (**ESB**) – Serving the capital city, ESB offers domestic and international flights, with connections to European and Middle Eastern hubs.
- **Antalya Airport** (**AYT**) – A key airport for Turkey's Mediterranean coast, AYT handles large volumes of seasonal tourist traffic, especially from Europe, Russia, and the Middle East.
- **Izmir Adnan Menderes Airport** (**ADB**) – Located on the Aegean coast, this airport serves both domestic and international travelers, with frequent flights from major European cities.
- **Dalaman Airport** (**DLM**) **and Bodrum-Milas Airport** (**BJV**) – These airports serve popular southwestern resort areas and see

heavy seasonal traffic from the UK, Germany, and other European countries.

Turkey's flag carrier, **Turkish Airlines**, is one of the largest in the world in terms of destinations served. It offers direct flights from major U.S. cities such as New York (JFK), Chicago (ORD), Washington D.C. (IAD), and Miami (MIA), as well as from Toronto (YYZ) and Montreal (YUL) in Canada. In Europe, it connects to nearly every major city. Turkish Airlines also offers extensive links to Africa, the Middle East, Central Asia, and Southeast Asia.

Pegasus Airlines is Turkey's main low-cost carrier, flying to over 120 destinations, primarily across Europe, the Middle East, and Central Asia, often via Istanbul's Sabiha Gökçen Airport. Other carriers like AnadoluJet (a subsidiary of Turkish Airlines) and SunExpress specialize in domestic and short-haul international flights, especially to resort areas.

For travelers coming from farther afield, many major international airlines serve Turkey, including Emirates, Qatar Airways, Lufthansa, British Airways, Air France, KLM, and Aeroflot, offering connections via their respective hubs.

The most budget-friendly months to visit Turkey are generally **November through March**, outside of the summer high season and major holiday periods. Winter sees lower airfare and hotel prices, except during the Christmas/New Year's period. Spring (April–May) and autumn (September–October) are considered **shoulder seasons**—airfares are often more affordable than summer, yet weather remains pleasant. Summer (June–August) is peak season, especially for beach destinations, so flights and accommodations tend to be more expensive and book up quickly. Booking international tickets **2–4 months in advance** typically yields the best prices.

When to Visit?

Turkey offers a wide range of experiences year-round, but the best time to visit depends on whether you want ideal weather, fewer crowds, or specific seasonal activities and cultural events.

Weather-wise, the most favorable months to visit are **spring** (**April to June**) and **autumn** (**September to early November**). These periods bring mild to warm temperatures, sunny days, and comfortable evenings—perfect for exploring Istanbul, Cappadocia, and Turkey's archaeological sites without the extreme heat of summer. Summer (July and August) is hot and dry, especially in inland regions where temperatures can exceed 35°C (95°F), but the Aegean and Mediterranean coasts benefit from cooling sea breezes, making them prime beach destinations. Winter (December to February) is mild along the southern coast but cold in central and eastern regions, with heavy snowfall in places like Erzurum and Kars—ideal for skiing and winter sports. Cappadocia in winter offers unique, snow-dusted landscapes for hot-air balloon rides.

Crowd-wise, peak travel season runs from **June to August**, when European and Middle Eastern holidaymakers flock to Turkey's resorts and major cities. Prices for flights and accommodations are highest during this period. **Shoulder seasons**—spring and autumn—are considered the sweet spot, with pleasant weather, fewer tourists, and more affordable rates. The **off-season** (November to March) is the quietest, except during the New Year holidays and major festivals, when local tourism picks up.

Activities-wise, spring and autumn are ideal for sightseeing, hiking, hot-air ballooning in Cappadocia, and enjoying open-air archaeological sites like Ephesus and Troy. Summer is perfect for beach holidays, yachting along the Turquoise Coast, and attending seaside festivals. Winter is the season for skiing in resorts like Uludağ, Palandöken, and Erciyes, as well as for cozy city breaks in Istanbul with fewer crowds.

If you're drawn to **festivals**, Turkey's cultural calendar offers many unique events worth planning around. **Ramadan** (dates vary each year) is marked by evening feasts and festive street scenes, particularly in Istanbul. **Eid al-Fitr** (**Şeker Bayramı**) and **Eid al-Adha** (**Kurban Bayramı**) bring nationwide celebrations and family gatherings. The **Istanbul Tulip Festival** (April) transforms parks into vibrant floral displays, while the **International Istanbul Film Festival** (April) attracts cinephiles from around the globe. Summer highlights include the **Aspendos International Opera and Ballet Festival** (June–July), staged in a 2,000-year-old Roman theater. In Cappadocia, the **Hot Air Balloon Festival** offers breathtaking mass balloon launches against the region's surreal landscapes. Finally, **Republic Day** (October 29) fills cities with fireworks, parades, and concerts celebrating the founding of modern Turkey.

Do I Need a Visa?

Whether you need a visa to visit Turkey depends on your nationality and the purpose of your trip. Citizens of many countries—including the United States, Canada, the United Kingdom, much of Europe, Australia, New Zealand, and several Asian nations—can enter Turkey without a visa for short stays ranging from 30 to 90 days within a 180-day period, depending on bilateral agreements. Your passport must be valid for at least six months from the date you enter Turkey and should have at least one blank page for entry and exit stamps.

Some travelers who are not visa-exempt may be eligible for an e-Visa, which can be obtained online in minutes at the official Republic of Turkey e-Visa website. The e-Visa is typically valid for stays up to 90 days and costs around $50 USD (fees vary by nationality). It's recommended to apply at least a few days before travel, although many receive approval almost instantly.

If you are from a country not eligible for visa-free entry or an e-Visa, you'll need to apply for a visa in advance at a Turkish embassy or consulate in your home country. Requirements vary but usually include proof of accommodation, sufficient funds, a return ticket, and a completed application form.

For stays longer than your visa or visa-free allowance—such as for work, study, or residence—you'll need to apply for a long-term residence permit through Turkey's Directorate General of Migration Management.

Entry rules can change, so before booking your trip it's best to confirm the latest requirements with the nearest Turkish consulate or on the official Ministry of Foreign Affairs website at **https://www.mfa.gov.tr/default.en.mfa.**

How to Get Around

Getting around Turkey is straightforward, with a mix of modern public transport in cities, extensive intercity connections, and regional travel options.

For **long-distance travel**, the most popular and cost-effective option is Turkey's extensive **intercity bus network.** Major operators like Kamil Koç, Metro Turizm, and Pamukkale offer comfortable, air-conditioned coaches with free Wi-Fi and onboard refreshments. Buses connect nearly every town and city, and fares are generally affordable—expect to pay around $10–$25 USD for a 5–8-hour journey.

Turkey also has a growing **high-speed rail network**, with fast trains linking Ankara, Konya, and Eskişehir to Istanbul. More routes are being added, and trains are clean, punctual, and competitively priced (often $8–$25 USD depending on the route). Conventional trains also run to destinations like Izmir, Adana, and Eastern Anatolia, offering scenic, slower journeys.

Within major cities, **metro systems** operate in Istanbul, Ankara, and Izmir. Istanbul's metro, tram, and ferry services are integrated through the **Istanbulkart** travel card, making urban travel easy and affordable (a single trip is usually under $1 USD). City buses are also widespread but can be crowded during rush hour.

Taxis are common but should be metered—be cautious of unofficial taxis, especially in tourist areas. Ride-hailing apps like **BiTaksi** and **Uber**

(operating only with yellow taxis) are available in Istanbul and some other cities, offering more transparent pricing.

For regional exploration, **renting a car** can be useful, especially along the Mediterranean and Aegean coasts, Cappadocia, or Eastern Anatolia. Prices start around $30–$50 USD per day, but driving in large cities can be challenging due to traffic and parking limitations. Also, **domestic flights** are frequent and inexpensive, with Turkish Airlines, Pegasus Airlines, AnadoluJet, and SunExpress offering multiple daily connections between major cities. Given Turkey's size, flying can save significant travel time—for example, Istanbul to Antalya takes just over an hour by air versus 10–12 hours by bus.

In coastal and island regions, **ferries** connect towns along the Aegean and Mediterranean, as well as routes to Greek islands in summer. In Istanbul, ferries are both a scenic and practical way to cross between the European and Asian sides of the city.

HELPFUL TIPS

Monetary Advice

The official currency of Turkey is the Turkish lira (TRY). Exchange rates fluctuate, but as of 2025, $1 USD typically equals around ₺33–₺34, depending on market conditions. You can exchange currency at banks, authorized exchange offices (döviz bürosu), and airports—though airport rates are often less favorable. ATMs are widely available throughout the country and usually offer competitive exchange rates, especially if you use a debit card that waives foreign transaction fees.

Credit and debit cards are widely accepted in urban areas, hotels, restaurants, shops, and many tourist attractions. Visa and Mastercard are the most commonly used, while American Express is accepted at some establishments, though less frequently. In smaller towns, rural areas, or local markets, cash is preferred—so it's always smart to carry some lira for small purchases, tips, or transport. Notify your bank before traveling to avoid any security holds on your card.

Turkey uses only Turkish lira for transactions; foreign currencies like U.S. dollars or euros are generally not accepted for payment, though prices may occasionally be listed in them for tourists. In some resort towns and bazaars, vendors may accept euros or dollars, but exchange rates are usually less favorable than at banks or ATMs.

Bargaining is common in Turkey, particularly in bazaars, markets, and small souvenir shops. It's considered part of the shopping experience, especially for carpets, ceramics, jewelry, and handicrafts. Bargaining should be friendly and respectful—start by offering about 60–70% of the asking price and work toward a fair middle ground. In department stores, malls, and restaurants, prices are fixed and not negotiable.

Tipping in Turkey is appreciated and often expected for good service. In restaurants, a tip of 5–10% is standard, given in cash directly to the server if possible. In cafés, rounding up the bill or leaving small change is common. For hotel staff, tipping porters around ₺50–₺100 per bag (about $1.50–$3 USD) and housekeeping ₺50–₺100 (about $1.50–$3 USD) per day is customary. Taxi drivers do not expect tips, but rounding up the fare is polite. For tour guides, a tip of around ₺200–₺400 per person (about $6–$12 USD) is appreciated for excellent service. Carrying small lira notes and coins is handy for tipping, public restrooms, and minor purchases.

Turkish Hospitality

Turkish hospitality is legendary and deeply rooted in the country's cultural traditions, strong family values, and a centuries-old emphasis on generosity toward guests. Turkey is known worldwide for the warmth, kindness, and attentiveness of its people, who often go out of their way to make visitors feel welcome. Whether you're wandering through the vibrant streets of Istanbul, exploring a quiet village in Cappadocia, or relaxing in a coastal town along the Aegean, you're likely to be greeted with genuine smiles, friendly conversation, and an eagerness to help—even from strangers.

Hospitality in Turkey is often expressed through sharing food, drink, and time. Offering guests a cup of strong Turkish tea (çay) or coffee is a near-universal gesture of welcome, whether in someone's home, a shop, or even a small office. In more traditional settings, visitors may be invited to share a meal—often prepared with an abundance of dishes, from savory mezes to rich stews and desserts like baklava. It's common for shopkeepers in bazaars to offer tea before discussing a purchase, not only as a courtesy but as part of building trust and rapport. Time is also generously given; locals may stop what they're doing to walk you to your destination, offer travel tips, or share stories about their hometown.

Politeness and respect play a key role in Turkish social etiquette. A warm greeting—such as **"Merhaba"** (**hello**) or **"Selam"** (**hi**)—is appreciated, and saying **"Teşekkür ederim"** (**thank you**) goes a long way. When meeting someone for the first time, a handshake is common, though among friends and family, kisses on both cheeks or a light hug are typical. Standing up when an elder enters the room, using both hands when giving or receiving an item, and removing your shoes before entering a home are signs of good manners. Conversely, being overly loud in quiet settings like mosques, refusing offered food or drink without explanation, or showing the soles of your feet to someone may be considered impolite.

To show respect as a visitor, it's important to be mindful of local customs and traditions. Dress modestly when visiting mosques and remove your shoes before entering. Accept offers of tea or food when possible, as declining without reason may be perceived as dismissive. Learn and use a few Turkish phrases—it's seen as a sign of effort and goodwill. Be patient with the slower pace of service in some settings, as socializing is often as important as the transaction itself. Above all, approach interactions with genuine curiosity, humility, and openness; this not only honors Turkish culture but also ensures you experience the full depth of its celebrated hospitality.

CHAPTER 2

CUSTOMS

IN THIS CHAPTER

- Travelers Entering Turkey
- Customs Entitlements and Monetary Restrictions
- Restricted and Prohibited Items
- 5 Practical Tips to Know Before You Go

CHAPTER 2
CUSTOMS

Travelers Entering Turkey[1]

When traveling to Turkey, visitors must hold a valid passport with at least six months of validity remaining beyond their planned date of entry. Many nationalities, including citizens of the United States, Canada, the United Kingdom, Australia, and several EU countries, can enter Turkey for tourism or business purposes without a visa for stays of up to 90 days within a 180-day period. However, some travelers are required to obtain an **e-Visa** in advance, which can be easily applied for online through the official portal at **www.evisa.gov.tr**. The application is quick—usually taking just minutes—and the e-Visa is sent via email for printing or saving on your phone.

Travelers from countries not eligible for visa-free or e-Visa entry must apply for a visa through a Turkish embassy or consulate before traveling. Always confirm the most up-to-date entry requirements for your nationality before departure, as rules can change.

Upon arrival in Turkey, you'll pass through standard immigration and customs procedures. At immigration, you'll present your passport and visa (if required), and you may be asked for proof of onward or return travel, evidence of sufficient funds for your stay, and your accommodation details. Customs regulations are straightforward—most personal

1 https://www.mfa.gov.tr/visa-information-for-foreigners.en.mfa

items can be brought in duty-free, but there are restrictions on items like tobacco, alcohol, and cash over certain limits.

After clearing immigration, you'll proceed to baggage claim and then to customs. Random checks are possible, especially for travelers arriving from outside the region. Major airports such as Istanbul Airport (IST) and Sabiha Gökçen International Airport (SAW) are well-equipped with services including currency exchange desks, ATMs, SIM card kiosks, car rental counters, and multiple transportation options. These include metered yellow taxis, ride-hailing services like BiTaksi or Uber, and public transportation links such as airport buses and metro lines in certain cities.

While English is widely spoken in major tourist hubs, especially by those working in hotels, restaurants, and shops, Turkish is the official language. Learning a few basic phrases like "Merhaba" (hello) or "Teşekkür ederim" (thank you) can make a positive impression and enhance your interactions with locals.

ADDITIONAL INFORMATION

For the latest entry requirements, safety guidelines, and travel alerts, check reliable resources such as the Republic of Turkey Ministry of Foreign Affairs visa information page at **mfa.gov.tr** or the U.S. Department of State's Turkey travel advisory at **travel.state.gov**. These sources provide current details on visas, health requirements, and any regional advisories that may affect your trip.

Customs Entitlements and Monetary Restrictions

When entering Turkey, travelers should be aware of specific customs allowances and monetary regulations to ensure a hassle-free arrival. Below are the key guidelines on what you can and cannot bring into the country:

Currency Regulations

Turkey allows travelers to bring in unlimited amounts of foreign currency. However, if you are carrying **€10,000 (or the equivalent in other currencies)** or more—whether in cash, checks, or other monetary instruments—you must declare it to customs upon arrival. This rule applies to everyone, regardless of nationality, and is intended to prevent money laundering and other illicit financial activity. Failure to declare amounts above this threshold could result in fines or confiscation of funds.

Permitted Items: Personal belongings such as clothing, toiletries, cameras, laptops, mobile phones, and other personal-use items are generally exempt from customs duties if clearly intended for individual travel purposes.

Duty-Free Allowances (for non-residents arriving by air or sea)

Travelers entering Turkey can bring the following items duty-free:

Alcohol:

- Up to 1 liter of spirits over 22% alcohol, OR
- Up to 2 liters of alcoholic beverages under 22% (e.g., wine, liqueurs).

Tobacco:

- 200 cigarettes, OR
- 100 cigarillos, OR
- 50 cigars, OR
- 250g of pipe or rolling tobacco.

Other Goods:

Non-alcohol and non-tobacco items with a total value of up to €430 (about $470 USD) for air/sea arrivals, or €300 (about $330 USD) for land travelers. For travelers under 15 years old, the limit is €150 (about $165 USD).

Gifts and Souvenirs:

Gifts and souvenirs are allowed as long as they are within the value limits and clearly for personal use—not resale. Bringing in bulk quantities of identical goods (e.g., electronics, textiles, cosmetics) may raise questions about commercial intent and could lead to duties or confiscation.

Food:

Strict rules apply to animal-based products such as meat, dairy, and related foods—they are generally prohibited from non-EU countries due to health and safety regulations. Packaged snacks, coffee, tea, and non-perishable goods are typically allowed in small quantities for personal use but always verify current rules before traveling.

Electronics and Personal Devices:

Personal electronics, including cameras, phones, and laptops, are permitted duty-free if intended for personal use. Bringing in more than one of the same type of high-value electronic device may result in duties or customs inspection.

Cosmetics and Toiletries:

Allowed in normal travel-sized amounts for personal use. Bringing in large quantities of the same product could be interpreted as commercial and may be subject to customs review.

To avoid delays or fines, declare any large sums of money, stay within duty-free allowances, and limit goods to personal-use quantities. For up-to-date regulations, visit the **Turkish Trade Ministry's Customs Guidelines** at trade.gov.

Restricted and Prohibited Items

Turkey has specific rules regarding prohibited and restricted items for travelers. Knowing these guidelines helps avoid complications at customs and ensures compliance with local laws.

Prohibited Items include:

Illegal drugs and narcotics: Possession, use, or trafficking of illegal drugs, including marijuana, is strictly prohibited. Even small amounts can result in severe penalties, including fines, arrest, and imprisonment.

Firearms, ammunition, and explosives: Weapons of any kind, including guns, knives, and explosives, are banned unless you have a special permit issued by Turkish authorities.

Counterfeit goods: Importing counterfeit products such as fake clothing, electronics, handbags, and accessories is prohibited. Customs officers will confiscate these items, and legal penalties may apply.

Endangered species products: Items made from endangered animals, including ivory, certain furs, and specific leathers, are strictly banned. This includes jewelry, clothing, and accessories made from these materials.

Pornographic material: Importing or possessing pornography is prohibited and can result in confiscation and legal action.

Explosive chemicals and hazardous substances: Chemicals, flammable materials, or other hazardous substances that pose a safety risk are forbidden.

Restricted Items include:

Agricultural products: Fresh meat, dairy, fruits, and vegetables may be restricted to prevent the spread of diseases and pests. Some items require special permits or certification for import.

Pets: Dogs, cats, and other domestic animals can be imported with proper health certificates, vaccination records (including rabies), and sometimes quarantine approval. Exotic animals and wildlife are subject to additional restrictions and permits.

Medications: Prescription medicines for personal use are generally allowed, but controlled substances may require documentation, such as a doctor's prescription or health certificate.

Cultural artifacts and antiquities: Exporting or importing historical or cultural artifacts is restricted to protect Turkey's heritage. Special permits are required.

Alcohol and tobacco: Travelers can bring limited quantities for personal use, but exceeding these amounts may incur customs duties.

Items that violate customs rules may be confiscated. Travelers may face fines, legal action, or arrest depending on the severity of the offense. Bringing counterfeit goods, endangered species products, illegal drugs, or unlicensed medications can result in significant penalties, including seizure and potential criminal charges.

ADDITIONAL INFORMATION

For a complete, up-to-date list of prohibited and restricted items, visit the Turkish Customs Authority website at **https://www.trade.gov.tr/customs-formalities.**

Five Practical Tips to Know Before You Go

1. **Respect traditional meal times:** In Turkey, lunch is usually served between 12:30 PM and 2:00 PM, while dinner often starts around 7:00–8:00 PM. In smaller towns, restaurants may close briefly between lunch and dinner, so plan your meals accordingly.
2. **Dress modestly at religious sites:** When visiting mosques or other religious locations, both men and women should wear modest clothing. Women may be asked to cover their hair with a scarf, and shoes are always removed before entering a mosque.
3. **Tea and coffee culture:** Offering tea (çay) or Turkish coffee is a common gesture of hospitality. Accepting these drinks when offered is polite and can lead to friendly conversations with locals.
4. **Public behavior and gestures:** Physical affection in public is generally limited; keep displays of intimacy moderate. Avoid pointing your feet at people or religious objects, as this is considered disrespectful.
5. **Learn a few Turkish phrases:** While English is spoken in tourist areas, using simple phrases like merhaba (hello), teşekkür ederim (thank you), and lütfen (please) is appreciated and shows respect for local culture.

CHAPTER 3

CRIME IN TURKEY

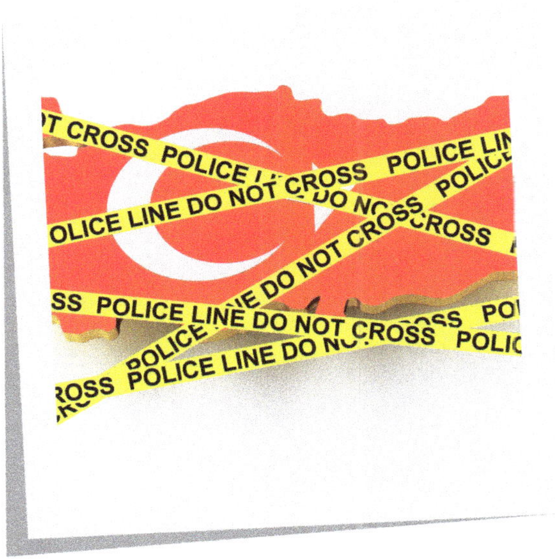

IN THIS CHAPTER

- Overview
- Crime Hotspots in Turkey
- Crime Statistics
- Quick Safety Tips

CHAPTER 3

CRIME IN TURKEY

Overview

Turkey is generally considered **moderately safe,** and the vast majority of visits to the country take place without serious incident. While crime exists, as it does in any large nation, it is often manageable and concentrated in particular contexts. Violent crime rates have gradually decreased over the past few decades, with the intentional homicide rate now relatively low compared to global averages. This long-term trend reflects improvements in public security and policing, even though year-to-year variations still occur.

For most travelers, the primary concern is not violent crime but **petty theft**. Pickpocketing, bag snatching, and scams can occur in crowded tourist areas. These incidents are opportunistic rather than targeted, and they are typically non-violent. Simple precautions such as securing valuables, being cautious in busy areas, and staying alert when using public transport are usually enough to avoid problems.

Another factor shaping Turkey's crime and safety landscape is the **risk of terrorism and regional instability.** The country has experienced incidents in major cities and tourist areas in the past, often linked to geopolitical tensions. While such attacks are far less frequent today, travelers are advised to remain aware of their surroundings, avoid demonstrations, and exercise extra caution in areas near the Syrian border, which carry elevated risks. The Turkish government maintains a visible law enforcement presence in urban centers and tourist destinations to deter such threats, which contributes to an overall sense of security for most visitors.

Contributing factors to crime in Turkey include the challenges of managing large urban populations, ongoing political dynamics, and the country's strategic position at the crossroads of Europe, Asia, and the Middle East. Despite these complexities, the overall experience for tourists is positive. Turkey's welcoming culture, strong hospitality traditions, and the importance placed on tourism as part of the national economy all reinforce a generally safe environment. For most travelers, being mindful of petty theft and following local guidance is sufficient to ensure a smooth and enjoyable visit.

Crime Hotspots in Turkey

In Turkey, crime hotspots are largely concentrated in areas that attract large numbers of visitors or where there are ongoing regional security concerns. In Istanbul, the country's largest and most visited city, places such as the **Grand Bazaar, the Spice Bazaar, Istiklal Street,** and **Taksim Square** are particularly known for pickpocketing, bag snatching, and various scams targeting tourists. Crowded **public transportation** and busy **ferry terminals** are also places where opportunistic theft occurs more frequently. While these crimes are non-violent, they can be frustrating and disruptive, making it important for travelers to stay vigilant with their belongings. In addition, taxi overcharging and tourist-focused scams are more likely in high-traffic areas, especially near airports, hotels, and major attractions.

Beyond petty crime, Turkey's **southeastern provinces** near the Syrian and Iraqi borders present different kinds of risks. Regions such as **Şırnak, Hakkâri**, and **areas close to the Syrian border** have faced instability due to terrorism, armed conflict, and cross-border violence. These areas are not typical tourist destinations, but they are important to note, as travel there is strongly discouraged. Even in major cities like Istanbul and Ankara, political demonstrations can erupt unexpectedly and sometimes escalate into confrontations with security forces, which is why avoiding large gatherings is generally the safest course of action.

When comparing Turkey's crime landscape internationally, the country generally experiences lower levels of violent crime than the United States. Travelers in Turkey are far less likely to encounter issues such as gun violence or random assaults, which remain more common in U.S. cities. Instead, the risks in Turkey are more likely to involve opportunistic street theft, scams in tourist-heavy districts, or region-specific instability in the southeast. For most visitors who remain in well-traveled areas and take standard precautions—like securing valuables, using licensed taxis, and being aware of surroundings—Turkey offers a safe and welcoming travel experience.

Crime Statistics

As discussed above, Turkey's most common crimes tend to be non-violent and opportunistic in nature. **Petty theft**, including pickpocketing, bag snatching, and scams targeting tourists, are by far the most widespread issues in crowded public areas. **Drug-related crimes**—particularly involving marijuana and synthetic cannabinoids—are increasing in cities like Istanbul, posing concerns for local communities, though they seldom involve tourists. **Domestic violence**, including femicide, also remains a serious social problem.

The intentional homicide rate in Turkey has shown a gradual decline in recent years. It stood at approximately **2.5 per 100,000 inhabitants in 2021**, down from around **4 per 100,000** in the early 2000s—demonstrating a long-term improvement in addressing violent crime. By comparison, Turkey fares much safer than the United States across several crime metrics. Turkey has fewer privately owned firearms per capita, a significantly lower murder rate, and far fewer crimes involving sexual assault. For tourists specifically, violent crimes are rare; the more common issues are petty theft and scams.

Corruption remains a challenge in Turkey. The country scored **34** on the 2024 Transparency International Corruption Perceptions Index, placing it well below the global average and signaling ongoing weaknesses in law enforcement transparency. While there are active anti-corruption laws, their enforcement is often inconsistent, which can affect public trust and crime reporting.

Nevertheless, overall, most travelers are unlikely to encounter serious crime during their visit to Turkey. While opportunistic street crimes and occasional security events do occur, violent incidents involving tourists are very rare. Staying aware of your surroundings, using common-sense precautions, and avoiding high-risk zones—especially near conflict-prone border areas—are usually enough to ensure a safe, enjoyable stay.

Quick Safety Tips

- Keep valuables secure and avoid carrying large amounts of cash. Use money belts or crossbody bags with zippers, especially in crowded places like bazaars, metro stations, and tourist sites.
- Be alert to common scams, such as overly friendly strangers offering unsolicited help, invitations to bars or shops, or taxi drivers who refuse to use the meter. Always use official taxis or ride-hailing apps.
- Respect local customs and dress modestly when visiting mosques or rural areas. Covering shoulders and knees is both respectful and can help you blend in more easily.
- Avoid political gatherings or demonstrations, as they can sometimes become unpredictable. Stick to tourist areas and follow local news updates when traveling.
- At night, use well-lit streets and official transport options. While violent crime is rare, sticking to safer routes reduces risks, particularly in big cities.

CHAPTER 4

CRIMINAL LAW VIOLATIONS

IN THIS CHAPTER

- Marijuana and Other Drugs in Turkey
- Prescription Medication
- Penalties
- General Questions
- Law of the Land Hypothetical
- Takeaways

CHAPTER 4

CRIMINAL LAW VIOLATIONS

Marijuana and Other Drugs in Turkey

Turkey has a long, complex history with cannabis. Evidence suggests cultivation dates back to as early as 1000 BC, where it was used for fiber, medicine, and textiles. During the Ottoman era, cannabis—especially hemp—was utilized in folk medicine and daily life, though it wasn't heavily regulated. Over time, especially in the 20th century, Turkey adopted stricter laws, eliminating most traditional uses and aligning with international drug control frameworks.

Today, **recreational cannabis remains illegal** in Turkey. Possession, use, cultivation—even in small amounts—is subject to **serious legal penalties**, typically imprisonment ranging from **2 to 5 years**, with courts often offering alternatives like treatment or probation for first-time offenders. Repeat offenses, trafficking, or cultivation can result in sentences of **10 to 20 years or more**—there are no "soft" allowances for tourists or residents.

In terms of **medical cannabis**, Turkey has introduced very limited reforms. Since 2016, certain prescription medications—like Sativex, a sublingual cannabinoid—have been allowed under strict medical supervision. In 2025, regulations advanced further with Decree Law No. 663, permitting pharmacies to sell **low-THC (under 0.3%) cannabis-derived products** with proper licensing. These products are tightly controlled and intended only for therapeutic purposes, not for general use.

Cultivation for medical and scientific purposes is **legally permitted**, but only under strict regulation. Since 2024, Turkey has authorized the growing of cannabis in select provinces for pharmaceutical active ingredients—overseen by the Ministries of Health and Agriculture. Industrial hemp (non-psychoactive) is also permitted but strictly monitored. However, **synthetic cannabinoids**, such as "Spice" (known locally as *bonzai*), are strictly **illegal** in Turkey. These substances were officially banned in 2011, reflecting the government's position against emerging designer drugs.

If you're a visitor with a valid medical cannabis prescription from your home country, bear in mind that despite some embassy correspondence suggesting otherwise, entering Turkey with such medication is **highly risky**. Turkish law applies uniformly—foreign prescriptions are generally **not exempt**, and customs does not recognize them for cannabis-based products.

Strict enforcement, severe penalties, and limited exceptions make Turkey one of the more conservative countries globally regarding drug policy.

Prescription Medication

Travelers to Turkey are **generally allowed** to bring **prescription medication for personal use**, but there are important rules and limitations to follow. Medications should be kept in their original packaging with clear labels showing the drug name, dosage, and prescribing doctor. It is also strongly recommended to carry a copy of your prescription and a doctor's note explaining the medical need, especially for controlled substances. The quantity you bring should match the duration of your stay, with up to a three-month supply generally considered acceptable.

Certain medications, such as opioids, stimulants, or some anxiety medications, may require **prior authorization** from Turkish health authorities. Over-the-counter medications are usually allowed in small, personal-use quantities, but some—like products containing codeine or pseudoephedrine—may be restricted or require documentation. Failure to declare controlled substances, bringing large quantities without proper paperwork, or attempting to import restricted drugs can result in confiscation, fines, or more serious legal consequences.

To avoid issues, keep all medications in your carry-on luggage, check in advance whether your medication is considered controlled in Turkey, and ensure you have supporting documents for any prescription or restricted drugs. Official guidance on prescription and over-the-counter medications can be found through the **Turkish Ministry of Health**, which provides information on controlled substances, medical documentation requirements, and import regulations for prescription drugs at **https://www.saglik.gov.tr**. In addition, **Turkish Customs** also outlines what medications can be brought into the country, the required documentation, and any quantity restrictions, available at **https://www.ticaret.gov.tr/gumruk.** Taking these steps helps ensure a smooth entry and prevents potential complications during your trip.

Penalties

In Turkey, the legal penalties for drug-related offenses vary significantly depending on the type of substance, the quantity, and whether the offense occurs in public or private. For **marijuana, possession** for personal use is illegal and can lead to **imprisonment ranging from one to two years,** along with fines. Penalties are more severe if the offense occurs in a public place, as this is considered an aggravating circumstance. **Cultivation or possession in larger amounts** is treated as evidence of intent to distribute, which can result in **prison sentences ranging from five to twelve years**, depending on the quantity and circumstances.

Distribution, trafficking, or large-scale cultivation of marijuana is treated as a serious criminal offense. Sentences for **trafficking** can range **from five to twenty years in prison**, and fines can be substantial. In cases involving organized crime, minors, or locations near schools, penalties are even harsher. **Synthetic cannabinoids** and other synthetic drugs are considered particularly dangerous, and their possession, sale, or production carries penalties similar to or even stricter than those for marijuana trafficking, often resulting in longer prison terms.

Possession or trafficking of other illicit substances, including cocaine, heroin, methamphetamines, and ecstasy, is treated with severe legal consequences. Even small amounts for personal use can lead to imprisonment of one to two years, while trafficking or intent to sell results in sentences of five to twenty years, potentially longer under aggravating conditions. Turkish law generally does not distinguish leniently between private and public use for hard drugs, and enforcement is strict, reflecting the country's **zero-tolerance approach** toward illegal narcotics.

General Questions

1. ***Is cannabis legal in Turkey?*** Cannabis is **illegal for recreational use** in Turkey, and possession, consumption, trafficking, or home cultivation can result in severe legal penalties, including imprisonment. However, **medical use** of certain cannabis-derived products has been **legalized under strict regulations.** Since 2016, sublingual cannabinoid medications like Sativex have been allowed with a doctor's prescription, and in 2025, Decree Law No. 663 permitted medical cannabis products with less than 0.3% THC to be distributed through pharmacies. Cultivation for medicinal and scientific purposes is legal in 19 provinces with official permission, but personal or home cultivation remains prohibited.

2. ***Where can I legally purchase marijuana in Turkey?*** In Turkey, the legal purchase of cannabis is restricted to medical use only and the low-THC cannabis-derived products (containing less than 0.3% THC) can be purchased in licensed pharmacies, strictly with a doctor's prescription . The Ministry of Health oversees the regulation, licensing, and distribution of these products, ensuring they are sold exclusively through authorized pharmacies . It is important to note that recreational cannabis use remains illegal in Turkey, and there are no legal avenues for purchasing cannabis for non-medical purposes.

3. ***Can I have marijuana on my person or in my hotel room in Turkey?*** In Turkey, possession of marijuana for recreational use is **illegal**, even in private spaces like hotel rooms. Having cannabis on your person or in your accommodation can lead to criminal charges, fines, and potential imprisonment. Only medically prescribed low-THC cannabis products obtained through licensed pharmacies are legally allowed, and these must be used strictly according to the prescription. Recreational use, personal possession, or cultivation is not permitted under Turkish law.

4. ***Are there any exceptions to the possession and consumption of cannabis in Turkey?*** **Yes.** The main exceptions in Turkey are for **medical use.** Patients can legally access low-THC cannabis-based medications with a prescription from a licensed doctor and through authorized pharmacies. These products must be used strictly as directed. Recreational use, possession without a prescription, and cultivation remain illegal, and there are no exceptions for personal or private consumption outside the medical context.

5. ***What are the penalties for possessing and consuming other types of illicit drugs in Turkey?*** In Turkey, penalties for possessing or consuming illicit drugs other than cannabis are severe. Possession of even small amounts of substances like cocaine, heroin, methamphetamines, or ecstasy is treated as a criminal offense and can lead to prison sentences, fines, and mandatory rehabilitation programs. The law distinguishes between personal use and trafficking, but enforcement is strict: if authorities suspect intent to distribute, sentences can be much longer, sometimes exceeding 10 years, especially in cases involving organized crime, minors, or large quantities. Public use or possession can also result in additional fines and legal consequences.

Law of the Land Hypothetical

HYPOTHETICAL: *Selin, a tourist from Europe, arrives at Istanbul Airport and unknowingly has a small amount of ecstasy in her luggage, unaware it was there. During a routine baggage scan at customs, airport authorities discover the drugs. Selin is immediately questioned and detained for further investigation. What penalties could Selin face for unintentionally possessing a controlled substance like ecstasy in Turkey, and how does the legal system treat such cases?*

ANSWER: *Turkey enforces strict anti-drug laws, and all hard drugs—including ecstasy—are illegal. Even if possession is unintentional, Selin can still be arrested and detained. Authorities will involve the prosecutor, and the case could lead to formal criminal charges. Penalties may include significant fines, imprisonment, or both. The law treats all possession seriously, and intent to sell is often considered separately from the act of possession, but unintentional possession at entry points like airports may still be prosecuted. Ignorance of the law is not a defense, and being a foreign national may result in extended detention or possible deportation after serving any imposed penalties. Securing legal counsel immediately is crucial in such situations to navigate the court process effectively.*

Takeaways

Recreational cannabis is **illegal** in Turkey, and possession, use, or cultivation—even in small amounts—can result in severe penalties, including imprisonment. Medical use is **highly restricted**, limited to low-THC cannabis products prescribed and dispensed through licensed pharmacies.

Travelers can bring prescription medication for **personal use** if it is properly documented, labeled, and matches the duration of stay. Controlled substances may require prior authorization, and failure to comply can lead to confiscation, fines, or criminal consequences.

Possession, trafficking, or cultivation of cannabis and other illicit drugs carries **significant legal consequences**. Penalties vary by substance, quantity, and context, with public offenses or trafficking attracting harsher sentences. Synthetic cannabinoids and hard drugs are treated particularly severely.

- The only legal exception for cannabis in Turkey is for medical use under strict supervision. Personal or recreational use, possession without a prescription, and home cultivation remain illegal, and foreign prescriptions are generally not recognized.
- Turkey enforces drug laws rigorously, including unintentional possession. Tourists or residents caught with controlled substances—even unknowingly—can face arrest, fines, imprisonment, or deportation. Legal counsel is critical in navigating these cases, as ignorance of the law is not a defense.

CHAPTER 5

ALCOHOL-RELATED OFFENSES

IN THIS CHAPTER

- Alcohol-Related Offenses
- Alcohol Regulation
- Things to Remember
- General Questions
- Law of the Land Hypothetical
- Takeaways

CHAPTER 5
ALCOHOL-RELATED OFFENSES

Alcohol-Related Offenses

Alcohol has a complex cultural history in Turkey, shaped by centuries of Islamic influence and Ottoman traditions, where alcohol consumption was often restricted but not entirely prohibited. Today, alcohol occupies a nuanced role in everyday life: while Turkey is a predominantly Muslim country, drinking is socially accepted in many urban areas, restaurants, and tourist destinations, though public intoxication is frowned upon and certain conservative regions maintain stricter social norms.

Typical beverages include **raki**, an anise-flavored spirit often referred to as the national drink, usually consumed with meze (small dishes) and during social gatherings. **Beer** and **wine** are also popular, particularly among younger generations and in cosmopolitan cities like Istanbul, Izmir, and Ankara. Wine production has a long history in Turkey, with regional varieties from Anatolia gaining international recognition, while imported wines and beers are widely available in urban centers.

Alcohol is **legal** and **commercially available** throughout Turkey for adults over 18, but sales are regulated. Retail stores and licensed venues must adhere to government rules, including restricted sales hours in some provinces, and strict labeling and taxation laws. Despite legality, cultural and religious norms influence consumption patterns, making moderate drinking the social standard in most settings.

Alcohol Regulation

The **legal drinking age** is **18**, applying to both purchasing and public consumption. Licensed venues like bars, restaurants, and nightclubs may serve alcohol, while retail stores and supermarkets are allowed to sell it under government restrictions, including bans on sales near schools and regulated operating hours in certain provinces.

Advertising of alcohol is **restricted**: broadcast media, including TV and radio, cannot run alcohol ads during daytime hours, and marketing to minors is strictly prohibited. Print and online ads are also subject to limitations, particularly regarding targeting young audiences or promoting excessive consumption.

Enforcement is carried out by local and national authorities, including **police** and **municipal inspectors.** Violations—such as selling to minors, unlicensed sales, or illegal advertising—can result in fines, temporary closure of businesses, and, in severe cases, criminal charges. Public intoxication is socially discouraged and may lead to police intervention, while **driving under the influence** is treated seriously: the legal blood alcohol limit is **0.05%** for most drivers and **0.00%** for commercial and novice drivers, with penalties including fines, license suspension, or imprisonment for repeat or severe offenses.

Things to Remember

- **Drinking Age:** 18 years old.
- **ID:** Government-issued ID is required to purchase alcohol.
- **Public consumption:** Drinking alcohol in public spaces, including streets, parks, or beaches, is generally prohibited and may attract fines or police intervention. Carrying open containers in public is also illegal.

- **Public drunkenness:** Public intoxication can lead to police intervention, fines, and in severe cases, temporary detention.
- **Drunk Driving:** Legal blood alcohol limit is 0.05% for most drivers and 0.00% for commercial or novice drivers. Penalties include fines, license suspension, and imprisonment for severe or repeated offenses.
- **Purchase of alcohol:** Legal at licensed bars, restaurants, nightclubs, and retail stores. Certain regions restrict sales near schools and during specific hours. Selling to minors is illegal and heavily penalized.
- **Alcohol Permits:** Permits may be required for serving alcohol at large public events or private parties in licensed venues; rules vary by municipality.
- **Illegal Alcohol:** Unlicensed or counterfeit alcohol is a concern; consuming illicit alcohol can lead to serious health risks and legal penalties.

General Questions

1. ***Can I drink and drive in Turkey?*** **No.** You **cannot drink and drive in Turkey**. The legal blood alcohol limit is **0.05%** for most drivers and **0.00%** for commercial drivers or novice drivers. Driving under the influence can lead to **fines, license suspension, and imprisonment** in severe or repeated cases. Authorities strictly enforce these laws, and penalties increase if alcohol contributes to an accident or endangers public safety.

2. ***Can I possess an open container in public?*** **No.** Possessing or drinking from an open container of alcohol in public is **generally prohibited** in Turkey. Public consumption of alcohol is restricted, and doing so can lead to **fines, warnings, or police intervention**, especially in city centers or near schools, religious sites, and government buildings. Enforcement may vary by region, but it is safest to consume alcohol only in licensed venues, private spaces, or designated areas.

Law of the Land Hypothetical

HYPOTHETICAL: *A group of friends rents a villa in Antalya for a vacation. They host a private party in the evening, serving wine, beer, and spirits. A neighbor, concerned about noise and drinking, calls the police. Are there legal restrictions for drinking alcohol at a private gathering in Turkey?*

ANSWER: **Yes.** *Alcohol consumption is legally permitted in private spaces, such as homes or rented villas. However, Turkish law also emphasizes public order and safety. If alcohol consumption or related noise is visible or audible in public areas, authorities can intervene. In this scenario, the police may issue a warning or a minor administrative fine for public disturbance. There are no criminal penalties as long as the drinking remains within private property and does not involve illegal activities like underage drinking or public indecency. Hosts should ensure that balconies or outdoor areas are not clearly visible from public streets or neighboring properties to avoid complications.*

Takeaways

The legal drinking age in Turkey is **18**, and ID is required to purchase alcohol. Sales are restricted near schools and may have regulated hours in some provinces. Selling to minors is illegal and heavily penalized.

Drinking alcohol in public spaces or carrying open containers is generally **prohibited.** Public intoxication can lead to fines, police intervention, or temporary detention, reflecting Turkey's emphasis on maintaining public order.

Turkey has strict DUI laws. The legal blood alcohol limit is **0.05% for most drivers** and **0.00% for commercial and novice drivers.** Penalties for violations include fines, license suspension, and possible imprisonment for severe or repeated offenses.

While Turkey is predominantly Muslim, alcohol is socially accepted in many urban areas, restaurants, and tourist destinations. Typical beverages include **raki, beer, and wine**, and moderate drinking in private or licensed venues is common. Excessive drinking or public drunkenness is socially frowned upon.

Alcohol advertising is restricted, particularly toward minors, and unlicensed sales or illegal promotion can lead to fines or closure of businesses. Authorities enforce laws through local police and municipal inspectors, ensuring compliance in public safety, sales, and consumption.

CHAPTER 6

FIREARM & AMMUNITION OFFENSES

IN THIS CHAPTER

- Current Firearm Status
- Firearm Restrictions for Visitors
- Penalties
- General Questions
- Law of the Land True Story
- Takeaways

CHAPTER 6

FIREARM & AMMUNITION OFFENSES

Current Firearm Status

In Turkey, firearm ownership is tightly regulated and only permitted under specific conditions. Turkish citizens who are **at least 21 years old** may apply for a firearm license, provided they have no criminal record, no history of mental illness, and no connections to organized crime. Licenses are issued by local authorities and recorded in a national firearm registry, and ownership must be justified by a valid reason such as **self-defense, hunting, or participation in sport shooting competitions.**

The types of firearms legally available to civilians are limited. Hunting rifles and shotguns are commonly permitted for licensed hunters, while handguns may be owned for self-defense under strict licensing conditions. Sport shooting firearms are allowed for individuals involved in shooting competitions. Fully automatic weapons, military-grade rifles, and other military-style firearms are **strictly prohibited**. The number of firearms a person may legally possess depends on the type of license they hold, with authorities specifying possession limits to prevent misuse.

To purchase a firearm in Turkey, individuals must hold a valid firearm license, complete safety and handling training, and pass a thorough background check confirming their eligibility. Firearms can only be acquired from licensed dealers, and private or unlicensed sales are illegal.

Carrying a firearm in public is **highly restricted**: firearms must be transported unloaded, locked in a secure case, and only while traveling to or from authorized activities, such as a shooting range, hunting trip, or sport shooting event. Concealed carry is rare and requires a special permit, which is seldom granted.

The use of firearms is also strictly regulated. Firearms may be used legally for hunting, sport shooting, or self-defense, but self-defense use is only lawful when it is absolutely necessary and proportionate to an immediate threat. Misuse of firearms, including illegal discharge, carrying without a license, or firing in public, can result in **severe penalties**, including **heavy fines, imprisonment, and revocation of the firearm license.** Overall, Turkey's firearm laws emphasize public safety, responsible ownership, and strict control, allowing firearms primarily for regulated sporting and defensive purposes rather than casual self-protection.

Firearm Restrictions for Visitors

In Turkey, firearm rights for non-citizens and visitors are **extremely limited.** Foreign nationals are generally **not permitted to purchase or carry firearms** while in the country unless they meet very specific and exceptional conditions, such as being part of an officially recognized shooting sports organization or holding a special permit issued by Turkish authorities. Tourists and short-term visitors are almost always **prohibited from bringing firearms into Turkey or acquiring them locally**.

Even if a foreign national qualifies for ownership under rare circumstances, they must comply with the same licensing requirements as Turkish citizens, including background checks, mental health evaluations, and justifying a legitimate reason for firearm possession, such as sport shooting or hunting under official supervision. Carrying firearms in public is strictly prohibited for non-citizens, and transporting a licensed firearm must follow the same regulations as for citizens: the weapon must be unloaded, securely stored, and only moved to or from an authorized activity.

Illegal possession or use of a firearm by a non-citizen carries serious consequences, including **detention, heavy fines, and possible deportation.** In practice, firearms in Turkey are considered highly regulated tools rather than personal defense items, and the laws reflect a strong emphasis on public safety, making access for non-citizens very restrictive.

Penalties

In Turkey, penalties for firearm-related offenses are strict and apply to both citizens and visitors, though consequences for non-citizens can include additional immigration-related consequences.

For citizens, illegal possession, carrying, or use of a firearm can result in severe penalties. Minor offenses, such as carrying a firearm without proper authorization, can lead to fines and temporary confiscation of the weapon. More serious violations—including illegal sales, possession of unlicensed firearms, or using a firearm in a crime—can carry prison sentences ranging from one to several years, depending on the severity of the offense. Use of a firearm in a violent crime or public disturbance can trigger longer imprisonment, along with permanent revocation of firearm licenses and confiscation of all weapons owned.

For visitors or non-citizens, the penalties are generally the same under criminal law but are compounded by immigration consequences. Possessing or carrying a firearm without proper authorization can result in arrest, prosecution, fines, imprisonment, and immediate deportation. Non-citizens may also be barred from reentering Turkey for a set period if convicted of a firearm-related crime. Even minor violations, such as carrying a firearm in a vehicle or public space without a permit, are treated very seriously for visitors, given that the laws assume non-citizens have no legitimate reason to possess weapons.

Overall, Turkey maintains a highly regulated approach to firearms, with strict penalties to discourage unauthorized possession or misuse, and non-citizens are under especially tight restrictions.

General Questions

1. ***What happens if the police catch me carrying a firearm in Turkey?*** If the police catch you carrying a firearm in Turkey without a valid license, the weapon will be confiscated and you may face fines, prosecution, and prison sentences ranging from one to several years; non-citizens can also be deported. Even if you have a license, violating rules—such as carrying a loaded firearm in public when only transport is allowed—can result in fines, temporary confiscation, or license revocation. Turkish authorities treat unauthorized firearm possession very seriously, and penalties escalate quickly, especially for visitors.

2. ***What is the potential sentence for a firearms violation upon conviction?*** In Turkey, the potential sentence for a firearms violation **depends on the severity of the offense.** Unlicensed possession or carrying of a firearm can lead to prison terms ranging from one to five years, with higher sentences for using a firearm in a crime, smuggling, or repeated offenses. Fines, confiscation of the weapon, and license revocation may also apply, and non-citizens can face deportation in addition to criminal penalties.

Law of the Land True Story[2]

In November 2024, Turkey's Interior Minister Ali Yerlikaya announced the results of the nationwide "Mercek-27" operation, a significant law enforcement initiative aimed at combating illegal firearm possession and trafficking across the country. The operation, conducted over the past week, led to the investigation of 1,664 suspects and the seizure

2 https://www.turkiyetoday.com/turkiye/turkiye-mercek-27-illegal-firearms-crackdown-75629

of 2,274 firearms, including 1,100 unlicensed pistols, 516 converted blank-firing guns, 26 long-barreled rifles, and 632 unlicensed hunting rifles.

The "Mercek-27" operation was part of Turkey's broader efforts to address the proliferation of unlicensed firearms, which have been linked to increased gun violence and public safety concerns. Interior Minister Yerlikaya emphasized the importance of prevention in combating illegal firearms, highlighting the need for collective efforts from citizens, civil society organizations, media, and local communities to reduce crime rates and improve public safety.

This operation underscores Turkey's commitment to enhancing public safety through proactive measures and collaborative efforts to address the challenges posed by unlicensed firearms.

Takeaways

Firearm ownership in Turkey is tightly regulated, with licenses granted only to citizens **over 21** who have no criminal record, no history of mental illness, and a valid reason such as hunting, sport shooting, or self-defense. Fully automatic and military-style firearms are strictly prohibited, and possession limits vary by license type.

Non-citizens and visitors face extremely limited access to firearms, generally restricted to official sport shooting or hunting permits under stringent supervision. Carrying or transporting firearms in public is almost entirely prohibited for foreigners, and illegal possession carries severe legal and immigration consequences.

To legally purchase a firearm, individuals must hold a valid license, pass background and mental health checks, complete safety training, and acquire weapons only from licensed dealers. Private sales of firearms are illegal.

Carrying and using firearms is strictly controlled: weapons must be transported unloaded in a secure case, and self-defense use is only legal when absolutely necessary and proportionate to an immediate threat. Misuse can result in fines, imprisonment, and license revocation.

Penalties for firearm offenses are severe. Citizens can face prison terms from one to several years for unlicensed possession, illegal use, or trafficking. Non-citizens face the same criminal penalties plus potential deportation and reentry bans.

CHAPTER 7

PROSTITUTION

IN THIS CHAPTER

- Overview
- Laws and Penalties
- Prostitution Practices
- Sex Trafficking and Exploitation
- Sex Tourism and Public Health Concerns
- Tips to Avoid Being Solicited
- Law of the Land True Story
- Takeaways

CHAPTER 7
PROSTITUTION

Overview

Prostitution in Turkey occupies a **semi-legal status**. The practice of selling sexual services is **legal under certain regulated conditions**, and state-licensed brothels operate under government oversight. Women who work in these establishments must be registered, undergo regular health checks, and hold official permits. However, activities outside of this system—such as street prostitution, escort services, pimping, or unlicensed brothel operations—are illegal and can result in fines or imprisonment. For men, purchasing sex from unlicensed workers is also punishable, though enforcement is uneven.

The root causes of prostitution in Turkey are tied to a mix of socio-economic and structural factors. Poverty, unemployment, and limited educational or professional opportunities often push women into sex work, particularly those from rural or marginalized communities. Migration also plays a key role, with some foreign nationals entering the trade due to economic hardship or coercion. Human trafficking remains a significant concern, as criminal networks exploit vulnerable individuals through deception, force, or debt bondage. For many involved, prostitution is less a matter of choice than a survival strategy in the absence of strong social safety nets.

Regulatory trends in Turkey have shifted toward tightening control over the sex trade, rather than expanding its legality. The number of state-regulated brothels has declined in recent years, and public debates increasingly frame prostitution in the context of morality, public order, and trafficking prevention. While some argue for better protection of sex workers' rights and safer working conditions, political and cultural pressures lean toward restriction. Campaigns against human trafficking and unlicensed prostitution have intensified, reflecting broader government efforts to limit informal sex work and combat organized crime linked to the industry.

Laws and Penalties

In Turkey, prostitution is addressed not by a single comprehensive prostitution law, but through a **patchwork of legislation and regulations** that distinguish between state-regulated sex work and illegal prostitution-related activities. As already mentioned, prostitution in Turkey is **legal but strictly regulated** under state oversight. The sale of sex is permitted only within government-licensed brothels, known as genelevs, which are authorized and monitored by local municipalities. Outside of this system, prostitution—including street work, escort services, or operating unlicensed brothels—is **illegal and subject to criminal penalties**. Third-party involvement, such as pimping, trafficking, or profiting from unlicensed prostitution, is also a crime under Turkish law.

There are officially designated areas for prostitution in Turkey, limited to the state-regulated brothels. These establishments are located in specific districts and operate under municipal permits. The government tightly regulates these brothels, requiring compliance with zoning restrictions, regular inspections, and strict adherence to public health and safety rules. Prostitution outside of these regulated areas is prohibited and often policed aggressively, especially in larger urban centers.

Sex workers who are registered in licensed brothels must meet certain requirements, including being over the age of 18, undergoing regular medical check-ups for sexually transmitted infections, and holding an official health card. They are also required to be Turkish citizens; foreign nationals are barred from working legally in this system. These requirements are intended both to regulate the profession and to monitor public health, though critics argue that they push many sex workers into unregulated and more dangerous conditions.

Penalties for prostitution infractions in Turkey vary depending on the nature of the violation. Unlicensed sex workers and clients engaging in prostitution outside the legal system can **face fines and administrative sanctions.** Those involved in organizing or profiting from illegal prostitution—including pimps, traffickers, or operators of unlicensed brothels—face far harsher penalties, often including **prison sentences.** Foreign nationals caught engaging in prostitution illegally may face **deportation in addition to criminal charges.** Enforcement has intensified in recent years as part of broader government efforts to combat human trafficking, protect public order, and reduce informal prostitution markets.

Prostitution Practices

Prostitution in Turkey is structured around a dual system of legality and prohibition that leaves most sex work outside the scope of state recognition. According to official records, around 3,000 women are registered and work legally in approximately 56 state-licensed brothels (*genelevler*), where activities are subject to strict health checks, regular police monitoring, and licensing rules. These licensed brothels are the only legal spaces in which prostitution can occur, and even within this system, restrictions are severe—only Turkish women who are unmarried and officially registered are permitted to work, while foreign nationals are categorically excluded. By contrast, the overwhelming majority of prostitution takes place outside this narrow legal framework, with estimates ranging between 100,000 and 150,000 sex workers nationwide. These unregistered workers, often including migrants, transgender people, and those pushed into informal arrangements, operate through street-based solicitation, private apartments, escort services, and increasingly digital platforms, which provide anonymity but also heightened risks of exploitation.

The attitude of local authorities toward prostitution reflects this legal divide. Licensed brothels continue to operate under heavy regulation, but in recent years, political and judicial decisions have led to the closure of many such establishments, effectively shrinking the already limited legal space for sex work. At the same time, law enforcement regularly cracks down on unlicensed prostitution through police raids, deportations of foreign workers, and charges against those accused of facilitating or profiting from sex work, such as landlords and pimps. While this enforcement-driven approach is justified on the grounds of combating human trafficking and protecting public morality, it has the effect of pushing the vast majority of prostitution underground. This underground nature makes sex workers far more vulnerable to violence, coercion, and health risks, as they lack legal protections, labor rights, or consistent access to medical services.

The overall pattern reveals a Turkish system that tolerates prostitution only under rigid, highly controlled circumstances, while actively repressing all other forms. Rather than recognizing sex work as a broader social and economic reality, the state maintains a restrictive and punitive framework that stigmatizes those working outside of licensed brothels. As licensed spaces decline, the number of sex workers operating illegally continues to rise, underscoring the limitations of a model that prioritizes control and containment over harm reduction, regulation, or worker protection. This approach reflects broader cultural and political attitudes in Turkey, where prostitution is seen not as a legitimate form of labor but as a moral and legal problem to be minimized and contained.

Sex Trafficking and Exploitation

Sex trafficking and exploitation are **serious concerns** in Turkey, shaped by the country's location at the crossroads of Europe and Asia, its role as a migration hub, and the presence of vulnerable populations such as refugees and economically disadvantaged groups. Each year, authorities identify hundreds of victims, many of whom are women and children. Both Turkish nationals and foreign migrants are affected, and traffickers often exploit individuals facing poverty, displacement, or lack of legal protections.

Certain areas of Turkey are particularly vulnerable to trafficking. **Border provinces** such as Şanlıurfa face heightened risks due to their proximity to conflict zones and the presence of refugee camps where oversight can be limited. **Major urban centers** like Istanbul also serve as hotspots, with neighborhoods that provide cover for criminal networks to operate across overlapping jurisdictions. Children living on the streets, as well as displaced women without stable housing or income, are among the groups most at risk of being coerced into prostitution or other forms of sexual exploitation.

The Turkish government has developed a strict legal framework and multiple institutional mechanisms to combat sex trafficking. National law prescribes heavy prison sentences for traffickers, and special provisions exist to punish those who exploit minors. Turkey has also established dedicated shelters, support services, and a 24-hour hotline for victims, while authorities carry out regular police operations to break up trafficking rings. Despite these measures, challenges remain in proactively identifying victims—particularly among refugee communities and other marginalized groups—making trafficking a persistent issue that requires ongoing vigilance.

Sex Tourism and Public Health

Sex tourism does exist in Turkey, though it is not as openly organized as in some other countries. It tends to be concentrated in major tourist hubs such as **Istanbul, Antalya, and Bodrum**, where international visitors are more numerous and nightlife infrastructure—including hotels, bars, and entertainment venues—facilitates access to sex services. While brothels and escort services operate legally under license, a significant portion of sex tourism occurs through informal or clandestine channels, often advertised online or via social networks and travel forums.

The organization of sex tourism is typically discreet. Licensed venues may offer adult entertainment as part of a broader hospitality experience, while informal arrangements often rely on word-of-mouth, digital platforms, or third-party intermediaries to connect tourists with sex workers. This discreet nature is reinforced by the fact that public solicitation outside licensed areas is restricted by law, so services are often mediated through private contacts rather than openly advertised on the streets.

Sex tourism in Turkey carries notable **public health concerns**. The transient and sometimes informal nature of the interactions increases risks for sexually transmitted infections (STIs) and limits consistent access to health screenings for both tourists and sex workers. Licensed sex workers undergo regular health checks, but those operating outside the regulated system may not, creating potential gaps in disease prevention. Authorities and NGOs sometimes run outreach programs in tourist areas to educate sex workers and the public about safe sexual practices, though challenges persist in fully addressing the health implications of sex tourism.

HELPFUL TIPS

Tips to Avoid Being Solicited

In Turkey, especially in busy tourist hubs like Istanbul, Antalya, or Bodrum, it is not uncommon for visitors to be approached or discreetly solicited, particularly around nightlife districts, bars, or entertainment venues. For travelers who wish to avoid such encounters, a few practical precautions can make a significant difference.

One of the most effective ways to avoid unwanted solicitation is to be mindful of where you spend your evenings. Certain nightlife areas are known for attracting sex work, and avoiding clubs, bars, or streets with reputations for such activity reduces the likelihood of being approached. Keeping to well-lit, family-friendly, or mainstream venues also helps minimize risk.

Behavior and appearance can also play a role. Tourists who appear intoxicated or overly open to strangers may be seen as easier targets. Maintaining a polite but firm distance from overly friendly strangers, declining offers for “special tours” or “companionship,” and avoiding prolonged eye contact with individuals loitering in solicitation areas are all useful strategies.

Finally, it helps to stay aware of scams. Some solicitation attempts may be linked to fraud or theft, where individuals lure tourists to overpriced clubs or attempt to extort money. If approached, the best response is to calmly but firmly decline and walk away. Staying alert, choosing social settings wisely, and avoiding vulnerable situations—such as being alone late at night in red-light areas—are the most reliable ways to prevent unwanted solicitation.

TRUE STORY Law of the Land Hypothetical [3]

In a significant law enforcement operation in Konya, Turkish police uncovered a criminal gang operating a massage parlor that concealed online as a legitimate business. Dubbed Operation "Kardelen," the probe revealed a disturbing scheme involving hidden-camera recordings of customers and the forcible coercion of individuals—women, children, and male employees—into prostitution through blackmail and the use of fabricated evidence. After months of detailed surveillance, police raided the establishment, detaining nine suspects. Out of these, five were arrested and sent to prison, while others were released under supervision. Investigators found evidence that victims were trapped through coercion, including psychological pressure and addiction to narcotics. The authorities noted that this case involved a complex criminal network using threats, surveillance, and manipulation to exploit vulnerable individuals.

This operation highlights Turkey's proactive response to organized and exploitative prostitution—not treating it merely as prostitution, but as a broader crime involving coercion, human trafficking, and psychological exploitation. The focus on dismantling these criminal

3 https://en.haberler.com/a-major-prostitution-operation-in-konya-21-18665352

structures reflects the government's strict stance against unlicensed and exploitative sex networks.

Takeaways

Prostitution in Turkey is legal only within state-licensed brothels (genelevs) under strict regulation, while all other forms of sex work—including street work, escort services, or unlicensed brothels—are illegal and penalized.

Licensed sex workers must be Turkish women over 18, registered, and subject to regular health checks, while foreign nationals are prohibited from working legally, pushing many into unregulated and unsafe markets.

The number of licensed brothels has fallen sharply, and authorities increasingly focus on shutting down informal sex work, a trend that drives most of the industry underground and heightens worker vulnerability.

Turkey's geographic position and large refugee population make it a hotspot for trafficking and exploitation, with border regions and big cities being particularly vulnerable.

While discreetly organized, sex tourism exists in tourist hubs like Istanbul and Antalya, raising concerns about sexually transmitted infections and limited access to consistent health screenings for unregulated workers.

CHAPTER 8

LGBTQ

IN THIS CHAPTER

- Homophobia in Turkey
- LGBTQ Legislation
- LGBTQ Tourism and Safety Concerns
- General Questions
- Law of the Land True Story

CHAPTER 8

LGBTQ

Homophobia in Turkey

Historically, Turkey's founder, Atatürk, established a secular framework in the early Republic that allowed homosexuality to remain legal—even as reforms addressed other social norms—though protections for LGBTQ+ individuals were not expanded. Despite **legality since the 1920s**, widespread homophobia persists, rooted in conservative cultural values, notions of masculinity, and religious influences that equate non-heteronormative identities with immorality or Western corruption.

Today, attitudes toward LGBTQ+ individuals in Turkey remain **largely negative**, especially in rural or conservative areas, where traditional family and gender norms strongly influence public sentiment. This is compounded by political rhetoric: for example, the ruling party has embraced anti-gender and homophobic messaging, positioning LGBTQ+ rights as a threat to societal values. These attitudes manifest in everyday life through various forms of discrimination. In educational and workplace contexts, LGBTQ+ individuals often conceal their identities due to the risk of ostracism or job loss. In some cases, proving one's homosexuality was once required to gain exemption from mandatory military service—forcing men to submit deeply personal evidence with no guarantee of privacy thereafter.[4]

4 https://fanack.com/turkey/human-rights-in-turkey/lgbtq-rights-turkey

Violence and discrimination against LGBTQ+ people are well-documented. **Digital hate** is alarmingly common: a report found that 90% of LGBTQ+ individuals in Turkey experience online harassment, stalking, doxxing, or hate campaigns. Public events like Pride marches are frequently banned or violently suppressed—one 2022 raid saw hundreds arrested, including minors, while journalists covering the event were also detained.[5] These bans and crackdowns continue today, reflecting institutional hostility.

Yet, there are visible voices of support and resistance. City councilor Sedef Çakmak became the first openly LGBTQ+ elected official in Turkey, advocating for gay rights within a major party. Activist and lawyer Yasemin Öz co-founded KAOS GL, a leading LGBTQ+ organization, and remains a prominent advocate for legal reform and freedom of expression. Likewise, artist Sezen Aksu and transgender legend Bülent Ersoy serve as gay icons and have used their platforms to challenge stigma.

On the legal and societal front, there's little progress. **No anti-discrimination laws** protect LGBTQ+ individuals, and s**ocietal stigma remains pervasive**, especially given anti-gender campaigns by state institutions and religious authorities. Istanbul Pride has been banned since 2015, and leaders continue to frame LGBTQ+ identities as antithetical to Turkey's "authentic" values. Despite the ban, LGBTQ+ activists continue to organize and attempt to hold Pride events each year, though they often face police intervention, arrests, and the use of force.

LGBTQ Legislation

Turkey's legal landscape regarding LGBTQ+ rights remains markedly restrictive and regressive. While homosexuality has never been criminalized, there are **no explicit protections** against discrimination based on sexual orientation or gender identity. Early efforts to include such protections in the Constitution—such as the February 2013 bill proposed

5 https://apnews.com/article/istanbul-pride-lgbtq-crackdown-515d46b4d73d84293e6a966dc2632b9e

by the opposition CHP to prevent workplace discrimination—failed to pass.[6]

Employment law in Turkey prohibits discrimination on grounds such as gender and "similar reasons." Although it doesn't explicitly mention LGBTQ+ status, courts have interpreted this to include sexual orientation and gender identity in some cases. Victims of such discrimination can seek compensation or administrative fines.[7]

Transgender individuals face particularly burdensome legal barriers when changing their legal gender. Under current law, gender recognition requires being over 18, unmarried, and submitting medical certification—typically necessitating sterilizing procedures. Though the Constitutional Court ruled against forced sterilization, in practice the requirement for surgery remains a de facto barrier. In 2025, a **draft law** proposed under Turkey's "Year of the Family" initiative signaled a sharp rollback of LGBTQ+ rights. The bill seeks to amend the Civil and Penal Codes to:

- Raise the minimum age for gender transition from 18 to 21,
- Reinstate medical criteria including "permanent infertility" as prerequisites,
- Criminalize public expressions of LGBTQ+ identity by framing them as "contrary to biological sex and public morality," punishable by imprisonment, and
- Impose prison terms for same-sex symbolic engagements or wedding ceremonies.[8]

Human rights groups have condemned the proposal, noting its alignment with anti-LGBTQ+ "propaganda" laws seen in authoritarian

6 https://en.wikipedia.org/wiki/LGBTQ_rights_in_Turkey

7 https://www.mondaq.com/turkey/employee-rights-labour-relations/1198600/lgbtq-employment-protection-in-turkey-what-is-the-law

8 https://www.turkishminute.com/2025/02/28/govt-proposes-law-restricting-gender-transition-criminalize-expression-of-lgbtq-identity3/

contexts like Russia and Hungary. The bill not only curtails fundamental freedoms but also deepens societal stigma by penalizing LGBTQ+ visibility.

LGBTQ Tourism and Safety Concerns

Despite its legal tolerance of homosexuality, Turkey remains a mixed environment for LGBTQ travelers. Major cities like Istanbul, İzmir, Bodrum, and Antalya are generally more accepting and offer discreet yet vibrant queer scenes. İstanbul's neighborhoods such as **Beyoğlu, Kadıköy, and Cihangir** boast LGBTQ-friendly cafés, clubs, and venues, including historic spaces like the Bigudi Club. **İzmir**, known as Turkey's most liberal city, hosts Pride marches and local government supports LGBTQ residents via initiatives like a dedicated municipal directorate. **Cappadocia** and **Bodrum** also attract LGBTQ tourists due to their stunning landscapes and laid-back, welcoming vibe.

However, public displays of affection (PDA) between LGBTQ visitors can still draw attention. Turkish culture generally discourages public displays of affection, even for heterosexual couples, so LGBTQ couples being openly affectionate—especially kissing—can be risky. A "don't ask, don't tell" approach, particularly in conservative or small-town settings, is often the safest route.

Safety-wise, LGBTQ travelers should take extra care. While same-sex relations are not criminalized, prejudice, harassment, and even violence remain real threats, especially if public identity is visible. Digital harassment and offline discrimination are also concerns—reaching out to local LGBTQ support groups like KAOS GL or SPoD can offer both guidance and community backing.

General Questions

1. ***Do laws in Turkey protect homosexual expressions and conduct?*** **No.** While homosexuality is not criminalized, and same-sex sexual activity between consenting adults has been legal since the foundation of the Republic in 1923, there are no specific anti-discrimination laws that explicitly protect LGBTQ+ individuals from discrimination or harassment based on sexual orientation or gender identity. The Turkish Constitution guarantees equality before the law, but it does not include sexual orientation or gender identity as protected categories.

2. ***What is the punishment for homosexual expressions and conduct?*** There is **no legal punishment for private homosexual conduct** in Turkey, as same-sex sexual activity between consenting adults has been legal since 1923. However, the situation is complicated when it comes to **public expressions of homosexuality**, such as holding hands, kissing, or participating in Pride marches. While these acts are not criminalized under Turkish law, authorities often use **"public morality" or "indecency" provisions** in the Penal Code or municipal regulations to restrict or punish them. In practice, this can result in fines, police harassment, bans on LGBTQ+ events, or detentions during demonstrations, as exemplified in the *Law of the Land True Story*.

Law of the Land True Story[9]

In late June 2025, Turkish police detained over 50 individuals—including activists, lawyers, and journalists—during an attempted

9 https://apnews.com/article/istanbul-pride-lgbtq-crackdown-515d46b4d73d84293e6a966dc2632b9e

procession for the Istanbul Pride march, which remains officially banned. Authorities imposed a sweeping police presence, blocked key gathering areas, and shifted the march location multiple times. Despite organizers' efforts to adapt, law enforcement swiftly arrested 54 people, with 47 remaining in police custody by evening. This continued a years-long campaign of suppression by the ruling party against public LGBTQ+ visibility.

The 2025 crackdown on Istanbul Pride highlights the broader challenges faced by LGBTQ+ rights in Turkey. Since 2015, the Istanbul Pride parade has been banned annually by the Istanbul Governor's Office, citing public safety concerns. Despite these bans, LGBTQ+ activists have continued organizing alternative events, often relocating to different neighborhoods to evade police detection. This crackdown forms part of a larger trend of diminishing civil liberties in Turkey, coinciding with restrictions on freedom of expression and assembly. For example, in 2024, authorities detained dozens of protesters advocating for women's rights, and in 2025, hundreds were detained during May Day protests. International human rights organizations such as Amnesty International and Human Rights Watch have condemned the Turkish government's actions, urging protection of LGBTQ+ rights and the cessation of unlawful detentions.

CHAPTER 9

SEXUALLY MOTIVATED/ VIOLENT CRIMES

IN THIS CHAPTER

- Overview
- Related Legislation
- General Questions
- Law of the Land True Story
- Takeaways

CHAPTER 9

SEXUALLY MOTIVATED/ VIOLENT CRIMES

Overview

Sexually motivated crimes remain a significant and deeply concerning issue in Turkey, affecting thousands of individuals each year. In 2023, over 190,000 cases of sexual offenses were investigated, reflecting both widespread prevalence and, in some cases, increased awareness and reporting efforts.[10] Child sexual abuse has been particularly alarming, with more than 30,000 children reported as victims in 2022, a three-fold increase compared to 2014, highlighting both rising incidents and the challenges in early intervention.[11] Women and children remain the most affected groups, with women experiencing high rates of intimate partner violence—approximately 38% have reported abuse during their lifetime.[12]

Social and cultural factors play a major role in sustaining these crimes. **Patriarchal norms** and **traditional gender roles** often normalize or obscure violence, while stigma and fear of social reprisal can prevent

10 https://stockholmcf.org/over-190000-sexual-offense-cases-were-investigated-in-turkey-in-2023

11 https://www.turkishminute.com/2023/09/20/more-than-30000-children-sexually-abused-in-turkey-in-2022

12 https://data.who.int/countries/792

victims from coming forward. Economic disparities, particularly in rural areas, exacerbate vulnerability, as poverty can limit access to education, legal resources, and social services that might otherwise offer protection. **Regional differences** are pronounced: southeastern provinces such as Diyarbakır and Şanlıurfa report higher-profile cases and show significant gaps in law enforcement responsiveness, while urban centers like Istanbul and Ankara offer comparatively more resources, reporting mechanisms, and shelters for victims, although challenges remain even in these areas.

Legal frameworks exist to criminalize sexual violence and provide protection, but **inconsistent enforcement and societal attitudes** often undermine their effectiveness. Additionally, **underreporting** remains a persistent problem, fueled by fear of stigma, family pressure, and distrust in authorities. Overall, sexually motivated crimes in Turkey are influenced by a complex interplay of social, cultural, economic, and institutional factors, making comprehensive reforms—including public education, stricter legal enforcement, and expanded victim support—critical for improving safety and accountability.

Related Legislation

In Turkey, sexually motivated crimes are addressed primarily under the **Turkish Penal Code (TPC)**, which criminalizes acts ranging from sexual assault to child abuse. **Articles 102 through 105** focus on **sexual assault and coercion**, prescribing penalties that vary depending on the severity of the offense and the victim's age. For instance, sexual assault against adults can result in imprisonment from **three to ten years**, while crimes involving children under 15 carry substantially higher penalties, sometimes exceeding 15 years. **Article 103** also criminalizes **sexual harassment**, including coercion, threats, or unwanted physical contact, with penalties of **one to three years** in prison.

Legislation provides additional protection in cases where the victim is particularly vulnerable, such as minors or individuals with disabilities. Child sexual abuse laws have been strengthened over the years, introducing longer sentences for repeat offenders and mandatory reporting requirements for professionals such as teachers and healthcare workers. The law also criminalizes the production, distribution, and possession of child sexual abuse material, with significant prison terms for violations.

Enforcement, however, has faced persistent challenges. Despite clear legal frameworks, **underreporting and societal stigma** often prevent victims from seeking justice. Many cases are dropped or result in minimal sentencing due to insufficient evidence or pressure on victims to remain silent. Law enforcement agencies and prosecutors sometimes lack specialized training in handling sexual violence cases, which can lead to mishandling or dismissal of complaints. Organizations such as the Turkish Ministry of Justice and various NGOs have been advocating for improved enforcement and victim support services, including specialized units for sexual assault cases within police departments and dedicated counseling services.

In recent years, reforms have focused on increasing protections for children and women, including raising awareness of consent and implementing stricter prison terms for severe offenses. However, **enforcement remains inconsistent** across regions. Urban areas like Istanbul and Ankara tend to have more resources and specialized services, whereas rural provinces often lack both legal and social infrastructure to adequately support victims. Thus overall, while Turkey has a comprehensive legislative framework to address sexually motivated crimes, cultural, social, and institutional barriers significantly limit its effectiveness in practice.

General Questions

1. ***Do laws in Turkey related to sex crimes protect the victims equally?*** **No.** While Turkey's laws criminalize sexual assault, harassment, and abuse, formally providing protection for all victims, with harsher penalties for offenses against minors and other vulnerable groups, in practice protection is unequal. Women,

children, and LGBTQ+ individuals often face social stigma, victim-blaming, and discrimination that discourage reporting, while authorities may treat cases involving marginalized groups less seriously. Enforcement also varies regionally: urban centers like Istanbul and Ankara have more resources and specialized units, whereas rural areas often lack trained personnel, leading to inconsistent application of protections and justice for victims.

2. ***Pursuant to law, what is the age of consent for sex in Turkey?*** In Turkey, the age of consent for sexual activity is **18 years old**. Sexual activity with anyone under this age is considered statutory rape and is punishable under Turkish criminal law, with stricter penalties if the victim is significantly younger or if the perpetrator is in a position of authority over the minor.

TRUE STORY

Law of the Land Hypothetical[13]

The case of İpek Er, an 18-year-old Kurdish woman from Batman, Turkey, tragically underscores the challenges in enforcing justice for sexual assault victims. In July 2020, Er accused Musa Orhan, a Turkish army sergeant, of abducting and raping her over several days. She reported the assault to authorities and consequently took her own life, leaving behind a letter detailing the abuse. Despite forensic evidence supporting her claims, Orhan was initially released under judicial supervision, leading to public outrage and protests demanding his arrest. He was eventually detained but was not imprisoned; instead, he was placed under house arrest with judicial control, a decision that sparked further criticism.

In December 2021, a Siirt court convicted Orhan of aggravated sexual assault, sentencing him to 10 years in prison, but did not order his immediate arrest, citing good behavior during the trial. This case has

13 https://medyanews.net/turkey-womens-rights-activists-demand-justice-four-years-after-death-of-ipek-er

become emblematic of the systemic issues within Turkey's legal system regarding the protection and justice for women, particularly in cases involving powerful institutions like the military. Women's rights activists continue to demand accountability and reform to ensure that such cases are handled with the seriousness and urgency they deserve.

Takeaways

Sexually motivated crimes are widespread in Turkey, with women and children being the most affected, and reporting remains hindered by stigma, fear, and cultural norms.

The Turkish Penal Code criminalizes sexual assault, harassment, and child abuse, with harsher penalties for minors and vulnerable groups, but enforcement is inconsistent.

Underreporting and societal pressures often prevent victims from seeking justice, especially in rural areas where resources and specialized services are limited.

Patriarchal norms, traditional gender roles, and economic disparities contribute significantly to the prevalence and underreporting of sexual crimes.

While legal reforms have strengthened protections, including mandatory reporting and stricter prison terms, comprehensive measures—public education, consistent enforcement, and victim support—remain critical for reducing sexual violence.

CHAPTER 10

ARRESTED IN TURKEY

IN THIS CHAPTER

- Overview
- Arrest Process and Rights of the Arrested Person
- Getting Legal Assistance
- Bail
- Complaints Against Police
- General Questions

CHAPTER 10
ARRESTED IN TURKEY

Overview

When traveling in a foreign country, it's imperative to recognize that you are subject to the legal jurisdiction and regulations of that nation. These laws may significantly differ from those in your home country and might not offer the same legal protections you are accustomed to. It's crucial to bear in mind that penalties for violating foreign laws can be more severe than those for similar offenses in your home country, and ignorance of these laws is not typically accepted as a defense.

The consequences for breaking the law while abroad can be severe and may include expulsion, fines, arrest, or imprisonment. Even unintentional violations can lead to serious legal repercussions. It is essential for travelers to be aware of and adhere to the laws of the host country to avoid legal entanglements and ensure a safe and enjoyable experience.

Specifically, stringent penalties are often enforced for possession, use, or trafficking of illegal drugs in many countries. Convicted offenders can expect severe consequences, including lengthy jail sentences and hefty fines. The legal processes for foreigners in the event of an arrest abroad involve being charged or indicted, prosecuted, potentially convicted and sentenced, and, if applicable, going through an appeals process.

Navigating a foreign legal system can be complex, and individuals arrested abroad must be prepared to comply with the legal procedures of the host country. Seeking legal representation and understanding the local legal nuances are crucial steps for those facing legal issues in a foreign jurisdiction.

Awareness of and adherence to the laws of a foreign country are paramount when traveling. Understanding the potential consequences for legal violations and being prepared to navigate the legal system of the host country are essential aspects of responsible international travel.

Arrest Process and Rights of the Arrested Person

In Turkey, the criminal justice system covers a wide range of offenses, including theft, assault, sexual offenses, drug-related crimes, public disorder offenses, and domestic violence, all prosecuted under the Turkish Penal Code. Law enforcement can initiate the arrest process when there is reasonable suspicion that an individual has committed a crime, and in urgent situations, authorities may detain a person without a warrant. Once arrested, individuals must be informed immediately of the reason for their detention and their rights in a way they can understand, which may include providing a translator if necessary. These rights include the **right to remain silent, the right to legal representation, and the right to be informed of the charges against them.** If the arrested person does not have a lawyer, the state must provide one free of charge, and the lawyer can be present during all interrogations and legal proceedings.

Suspects are generally held in police custody for **up to 24 hours**, after which they must be brought before a judge, who decides whether to release them, extend detention, or take other legal measures. For serious offenses such as terrorism, drug trafficking, or violent crimes, this period may be extended, **up to 48 hours** in certain cases. During detention, individuals have the right to a medical examination, either upon request or automatically if there are concerns about health or mistreatment. Interrogations must follow strict procedural rules, and any statements obtained under duress are inadmissible in court.

Foreign nationals have **additional protections**. They are entitled to contact their consulate or embassy, which can provide guidance, practical assistance, and visitation rights. They also have the right to a free interpreter if they do not speak Turkish, and all key documents must be translated into a language they understand. While arrest could have immigration consequences, such as affecting a residence permit, deportation cannot occur without due legal process.

Although Turkish law provides these safeguards on paper, in practice challenges such as **inconsistent enforcement, bureaucratic delays, and regional disparities** in resources can affect outcomes for both citizens and foreigners, particularly in rural areas compared to major cities like Istanbul or Ankara. These protections aim to ensure that all arrested persons, regardless of nationality, are treated fairly and have access to due process under Turkish law.

Getting Legal Assistance

To get qualified legal assistance in Turkey, you have several options whether you are a resident, visitor, or foreign national. If you can afford **private representation,** you can hire a lawyer directly, but note that all lawyers must be registered with a **Turkish Bar Association** to practice. Many larger cities such as Istanbul, Ankara, and Izmir have Bar Association offices where you can search for lawyers by specialty, and some firms advertise English-speaking or foreign-client services. Your embassy or consulate can also provide a list of local lawyers who are experienced in assisting foreigners.

If you cannot afford a lawyer, you are entitled to **free legal assistance** under Turkey's legal aid system, known as **"Adli Yardım."** This is administered through local Bar Associations. Foreigners can qualify if they cannot afford a lawyer and if there is reciprocity, meaning Turkish citizens would have similar access to aid in the foreigner's home country. Refugees, conditional refugees, and those under international protection do not need to meet this reciprocity requirement and may only be asked for a poverty certificate. If approved, your lawyer's fees and, in many cases, litigation costs will be covered by the state.

In criminal cases involving serious charges, juveniles, or persons with disabilities, a lawyer will be appointed automatically even if not requested.

If you are arrested in Turkey, you have the right to be informed immediately of the reasons for your detention in a language you understand. You have the right to remain silent and you should clearly state "Avukat istiyorum" ("I want a lawyer"). You do not have to answer questions until your lawyer is present. If you do not have the means to hire one, the Bar Association is required to appoint one for you free of charge from the moment of detention.

While your embassy or consulate cannot provide legal representation or interfere in court cases, but they play an important role in safeguarding your rights. They can give you a list of reliable local lawyers, check on your welfare while in custody, and, with your consent, notify your family or friends. Many embassies encourage you to contact them as soon as possible if you are arrested or detained in Turkey, since they can help ensure that you are treated fairly and that you remain in contact with legal support.

Bail

Turkey does not have a bail system in the same way that countries like the United States do, where money is paid to secure temporary release. Instead, Turkish law allows for "judicial control measures" as an alternative to detention. These measures can include conditions such as regularly reporting to the police, restrictions on travel, surrendering a passport, or a prohibition on leaving a certain residence or city. In some cases, the court may require a financial guarantee, but this is not the standard practice and is only one of several possible restrictions.

The decision on whether a person will be held in custody or released under judicial control is made by a judge after the initial detention period. The judge considers factors such as the seriousness of the offense, the risk of flight, and whether evidence could be tampered with. Judicial control can be imposed for both citizens and foreigners and may remain in place until trial.

For visitors, the biggest consideration is the risk of being seen as a flight risk. Because foreigners may not have strong ties to Turkey, courts are often more cautious and may prefer detention or strict conditions over simple release. In practice, this could mean surrendering your passport, restrictions on leaving the country, or more frequent reporting obligations. Having a local lawyer and embassy support is especially important in these cases, as they can argue that proper conditions are in place to ensure you comply with the judicial process.

Complaints Against Police

The overall reputation of the Turkish police is one of **persistent concern** among both domestic watchdogs and international observers. Allegations of excessive force, particularly during protests, have been widely reported. Human Rights Watch documented examples of ill-treatment, torture, shootings, and impunity for police violence, noting that investigations often lack independence and fail to hold officers accountable. Council of Europe officials have similarly highlighted systemic issues, condemning the improper use of tear gas and lack of safeguards during demonstrations.

Common complaints encompass excessive force in custody and during identity checks, torture, and an alarming rise in mistreatment during protests. Data from human rights groups report increases in complaints alleging sexual harassment, rape, beatings, verbal abuse, and death threats. The Turkish Human Rights Foundation (TİHV), for example, recorded widespread instances of police brutality during demonstrations and in detention centers, blaming weak oversight and cover-ups for a deteriorating rights environment.[14]

If your rights are violated by the police, formal complaints can be filed with the **Public Prosecutor's Office**, **police stations** themselves, or **through the provincial or district governorship**, which forwards the case to prosecutors. Complaints can be made orally or preferably

14 https://www.turkishminute.com/2023/08/29/complaint-alleging-police-mistreatment-increased-22-percent-in-turkey-in-2022

in writing, clearly describing the incident. When possible, include details like date, time, location, identities or badge numbers of officers, witness contacts, and any medical or photographic records. The written complaint may be submitted in person or electronically via Turkey's UYAP system using an e-signature.[15] You also have the right—under the Constitution—to petition any government authority and can submit complaints through CİMER (the Presidency's Communication Center).

Several organizations offer support or advocacy related to police complaints. The **Ombudsman Institution** (**Kamu Denetçiliği Kurumu**), an independent body answering only to Parliament, investigates complaints against administrative actions—including those by police. Foreign nationals may lodge complaints in writing (in Turkish or another language if justified) and can apply in person, by mail, email, or via provincial governorates. There are no fees for filing, and confidentiality can be requested. Complaints must generally be submitted within six months of a response from the administration.

The **Human Rights Foundation of Turkey** (**HRFT or** TİHV) provides treatment to torture survivors and documents human rights violations. It operates centers across Turkey—in Ankara, Istanbul, Izmir, Adana, and Diyarbakir—and can be contacted via email (tihv@tihv.org.tr, hrft@tihv.org.tr) or by phone or fax at its regional offices. **Mazlumder** (**Association for Human Rights and Solidarity for the Oppressed**) is another NGO that advocates for victims of oppression, including religious discrimination, and operates from Istanbul with branches across many provinces. While its primary focus is not police complaints per se, it may offer broader human rights support.

Additionally, there is a notable emergency hotline specifically in Istanbul managed by the Progressive Lawyers Association for victims of police violence. Known as **"İmdat Polis"** ("Help, Police!"), this 24/7 line dispatches volunteer lawyers immediately when an incident is reported, aiming to ensure on-site legal protection and documentation.

15 https://ballawfirm.com/en/turn-to-prosecution-in-turkey

General Questions

1. ***If I am convicted in Turkey, am I likely to be released on bail pending the outcome of my appeal?*** In Turkey, release on bail after conviction and while awaiting appeal is very rare. Although courts may grant bail or "judicial control" measures before trial, once convicted the sentence generally starts being executed immediately, and appeals do not automatically suspend detention. Judges may consider release only in exceptional cases—such as strong humanitarian grounds or compelling appeal prospects—but in practice, Turkish courts almost always keep convicted individuals in custody pending appeal.

2. ***Who is entitled to bail?*** In Turkey, bail (judicial control) can be granted to defendants before conviction if the court believes they are not a flight risk, won't tamper with evidence, and aren't likely to reoffend. Eligible individuals typically include those accused of less severe crimes, first-time offenders, or people with strong ties to the community. Certain serious offenses—like terrorism, organized crime, or violent felonies—usually make bail unlikely. After conviction, entitlement to bail is very limited and only considered in exceptional circumstances.

3. ***If I am arrested, how soon will I see a judge or magistrate?*** In Turkey, if you are arrested, you must be brought before a judge **within 24 hours.** During this hearing, the judge will decide whether to release you, place you under judicial control, or keep you in detention while the investigation continues. If the 24-hour period lapses without a hearing, the detention is considered unlawful.

4. ***Will I be able to contact my country's embassy in Turkey?*** **Yes.** If you are arrested in Turkey, you have the right to contact your country's embassy or consulate. Consular officials can provide assistance, such as explaining local legal procedures, helping you find a lawyer, and ensuring your rights are respected, but they cannot intervene in legal proceedings or secure your release.

CHAPTER 11

JAILS VS. PRISONS: CONDITIONS & CULTURE

IN THIS CHAPTER

- Overview
- Prison Conditions and Living Environment
- Inmate Rights and Legal Protections
- General Questions

CHAPTER 11

JAILS VS. PRISONS: CONDITIONS & CULTURE

Overview

Turkey's prison system is designed to balance security, punishment, and rehabilitation, operating under the **Ministry of Justice's General Directorate of Prisons and Detention Houses**. The system includes various facility types, such as high-security closed prisons, medium-security facilities, and open or semi-open prisons, which accommodate inmates based on the severity of their crimes and rehabilitation needs. In Turkey, the term **"jail"** is typically used for **short-term detention centers** (arrest or pre-trial), while **"prison"** refers to **facilities for convicted individuals** serving longer sentences. High-security prisons house serious offenders, limiting freedom and movement, whereas semi-open and open prisons provide inmates with more privileges, work opportunities, and gradual reintegration into society.

The Turkish prison system is governed by the **Turkish Penal Code and the Law on Execution of Sentences and Security Measures (Ceza ve Güvenlik Tedbirlerinin İnfazı Hakkında Kanun)**. This legal framework emphasizes not only detention but also social reintegration, education, and rehabilitation, although implementation varies widely across facilities. Prisons are operated under the **Ministry of Justice**, with each facility managed by a director and staff trained in correctional administration. Daily operations focus on security and order, but programs for education, vocational training, and psychological support are offered depending on resources. Inmates are classified based on crime severity, behavior, and rehabilitation potential.

Major challenges in the Turkish prison system include **overcrowding**, especially in high-security facilities, **limited resources for rehabilitation**, and **inconsistent access to mental health care**. Human rights organizations have highlighted concerns about detention conditions, access to medical care, and social reintegration opportunities.

Prison Conditions and Living Environment

In Turkey, prison facilities are classified primarily by security level: **high-security (closed)**, **medium-security**, and **open or semi-open prisons. Closed prisons** house inmates convicted of serious crimes and have the most restrictive conditions. Prisoners spend much of the day in their cells under close supervision, with limited access to work, education, or recreational activities. Overcrowding and tension can be significant in these facilities due to the strict confinement and nature of offenses. **Semi-open prisons** allow inmates more freedom within the facility and sometimes outside for work, education, or rehabilitation programs. Dormitory-style accommodations are common, and inmates generally have greater access to communal areas. These facilities serve as transitional spaces, preparing prisoners for reintegration into society. **Open prisons** have the most lenient conditions, with dormitory living and daily community access for work or training. Inmates are usually low-risk or nearing the end of their sentences, and the environment emphasizes personal responsibility and rehabilitation.

Healthcare access in Turkish prisons is available, but challenges remain. Although facilities have medical units and staff, overcrowding, limited resources, and uneven distribution of specialists can delay or restrict care. Chronic conditions, mental health needs, and emergency services may not always be adequately addressed.

As for **basic needs**, prisoners receive three meals a day, though the quality and variety can vary by facility. Sanitation standards also differ: inmates have access to showers, toilets, and basic hygiene supplies, but older buildings and overcrowding sometimes compromise cleanliness and maintenance. Basic needs are met, but the extent depends heavily on institutional resources and staffing.

Overall, Turkey's prison system faces ongoing challenges, including overcrowding, insufficient rehabilitation infrastructure, and uneven access to healthcare. While open and semi-open facilities aim to support reintegration and skill development, structural and operational limitations continue to affect living conditions across the country.

Inmate Rights and Legal Protections

In Turkey, prisoners are entitled to a range of **constitutional rights and legal protections**, though their enforcement can vary across facilities. The **Turkish Constitution** guarantees fundamental rights, including the right to life, physical integrity, dignity, and equality. **Article 17** prohibits torture and inhuman or degrading treatment, while **Article 36** ensures the right to legal defense and access to a fair trial. The **Law on Execution of Sentences and Security Measures** reinforces these protections, requiring prison authorities to safeguard inmates' health, safety, and dignity, and prohibiting abuse by staff or other prisoners.

Inmates have the right to access legal resources and appeal court decisions. They can request judicial review through Penitentiary Judges, submit complaints regarding detention conditions, and appeal to higher courts if they believe their rights have been violated. Legal aid is available for those who cannot afford a lawyer, although access may be limited in practice due to procedural delays or resource constraints.

Despite these protections, **issues of abuse and inadequate recourse persist.** Reports from human rights organizations, including Amnesty International and the CPT, have documented allegations of physical mistreatment, overcrowding-related stress, and limited access to independent legal counsel. While Turkish law provides mechanisms to report abuse—requiring prison administrators to inform judicial authorities—practical challenges such as slow investigations, bureaucratic obstacles, and insufficient oversight can hinder effective enforcement.

Thus, while Turkey has a legal framework aimed at protecting inmate rights, implementation remains uneven, and prisoners often face difficulties in fully exercising their legal protections, particularly in overcrowded or understaffed facilities.

General Questions

1. ***What is the difference between a jail and prison in Turkey?*** In Turkey, the main difference is purpose and duration of detention. Jails (often called "arrest or detention centers") hold individuals temporarily, usually before trial or while under investigation. They are for short-term confinement and focus primarily on security and processing detainees. Prisons, on the other hand, house convicted individuals serving sentences. They are designed for long-term detention, include varying security levels (closed, semi-open, open), and often provide rehabilitation programs alongside confinement.

2. ***Do jails and prisons offer religious services to inmates?*** **Yes.** In Turkey, both jails and prisons generally provide religious services for inmates, primarily reflecting the country's majority Muslim population. Facilities typically allow access to prayer rooms, imams, and Quran study, and inmates may participate in daily prayers and religious activities. Non-Muslim inmates can sometimes request access to religious materials or services, but availability may be more limited depending on the facility and local resources.

3. ***How do prisoners spend their time?*** In Turkish prisons, how inmates spend their time depends on the security level and available programs. In high-security (closed) prisons, much of the day is spent in cells, with limited movement, recreation, or interaction. In semi-open and open prisons, inmates have more freedom to participate in work programs, vocational training, education, and communal activities. All facilities typically allow meals, limited recreation, and some social time, while access to programs like counseling, religious activities, or sports varies by prison and resources.

4. ***What type of jobs can inmates perform?*** In Turkish prisons, inmates—particularly in semi-open and open facilities—can perform a variety of jobs both inside and outside the prison under supervision. Common work includes industrial or craft activities such as sewing, woodworking, metalwork, or manufacturing products for internal use or state contracts. Inmates may also engage in agricultural work like farming, animal care, or gardening on prison farms, as well as maintenance and cleaning tasks, including facility upkeep, kitchen work, laundry, and sanitation. Some prisoners may assist with administrative duties, such as clerical work or managing prison libraries. These jobs are designed to teach skills, provide a small income, and support reintegration into society after release, with availability depending on the prison type, security level, and individual eligibility.

5. ***How does the prison commissary system work in Turkey?*** In Turkey, the prison commissary system allows inmates to purchase basic personal items, food supplements, and hygiene products using money from their own funds or earnings from prison work. Each facility has a designated store stocked with approved goods, and inmates typically maintain an account managed by the prison administration. Family members can sometimes deposit money into this account to support purchases. Access and the range of available items vary by prison, and all transactions are closely monitored to prevent misuse or the circulation of unauthorized items.

6. ***What is prison culture in Turkey?*** Prison culture in Turkey is shaped by hierarchy, social norms, and survival dynamics within each facility. Relationships among inmates are influenced by factors such as age, criminal background, ethnicity, and length of sentence, with informal networks often forming for protection, support, or access to resources. Respect for established rules—both official and unwritten—is important for personal safety. Inmates often spend time in communal areas, engage in work or educational programs, and participate in religious or recreational activities, but social life can be tense, especially in overcrowded or high-security prisons.

CHAPTER 12

HELPING A FRIEND OR RELATIVE IMPRISONED IN TURKEY

IN THIS CHAPTER

- Overview
- Sending Food, Supplies, and Money to an Inmate
- Mail, Phone Calls, and Visitation
- Prison Scams
- Upon Release

CHAPTER 12

HELPING A FRIEND OR RELATIVE IMPRISONED IN TURKEY

Overview

If your family member or friend is imprisoned in Turkey, it is important to act quickly and understand what resources are available. The detained person should request that prison authorities notify the nearest embassy or consulate. Family members may also directly contact the **U.S. Embassy in Ankara** or the **Consulates General in Istanbul and Adana** to report the arrest. The embassy can assist by notifying family and friends, facilitating communication, monitoring the detainee's well-being, and providing information about the legal process and local attorneys. While they cannot intervene in court proceedings or secure release, they can help ensure that the detainee's rights are respected.

The embassy maintains a **list of English-speaking attorneys in Turkey**, including those in major cities such as Ankara, Istanbul, and Izmir. These lawyers are independent professionals and not endorsed by the embassy but are available to represent foreign nationals in criminal proceedings. This list can be accessed through the embassy's official legal assistance page at **https://tr.usembassy.gov/legal-assistance**. In exceptional situations, the U.S. government may provide limited financial support, such as loans for repatriation or medical emergencies.

Family members and friends can support detainees in Turkey in several ways. **Regular communication** is important—letters, scheduled phone calls, or video visits (when available) help maintain emotional stability. **Financial assistance** is also critical since inmates often rely on funds deposited in their commissary accounts to purchase food, hygiene products, and other essentials. For U.S. citizens, deposits can sometimes be facilitated through the embassy's OCS Trust system.

Visitation is allowed in most Turkish prisons but subject to strict rules. Visits usually require prior approval and valid identification. Personal visits can be very meaningful, and in some facilities, packages with approved items like clothing, books, or personal supplies may also be sent, though regulations vary and must be confirmed with the specific prison.

Finally, if you believe your loved one's rights are being violated, you may reach out to human rights organizations active in Turkey, such as the **Human Rights Association** (**İHD**) or international groups like **Amnesty International**, which monitor detention conditions and advocate against mistreatment.

Sending Food, Supplies, and Money to an Inmate

In Turkey, family and friends are generally **not allowed to bring or send homemade food directly** to inmates. Prisons provide daily meals, and inmates may supplement their diet by purchasing food and snacks through the **prison commissary**. In some cases, families may bring packaged, factory-sealed food items during scheduled visits, but this is subject to approval and strict inspection by prison authorities. Fresh or perishable foods, alcohol, and any items considered a security risk are strictly prohibited.

Packages can be sent, but they are **subject to tight regulations**. Each prison sets limits on the number and size of packages that inmates can receive, often restricted to a few times per year (such as during religious holidays). Packages must be sent through **approved postal services** or **delivered in person by registered family members**. Permitted items typically include clothing, books, and personal hygiene products, while banned items include electronics, sharp objects, drugs, and unauthorized documents. All packages are inspected before reaching the inmate.

Money can be sent to inmates by depositing funds into their **prison account** managed by the administration. Family members or friends can transfer money **via bank deposits, postal transfers, or direct payments at the prison cashier**, depending on the facility. The inmate can then use these funds to buy food, toiletries, stationery, and other essentials from the commissary. Depositors must usually provide the inmate's full name, prisoner number, and proof of relationship. Some facilities also restrict who may send money, limiting it to immediate family members or legal representatives.

Mail, Phone Calls, and Visitation

In Turkey, inmates are allowed to receive **mail**, including letters and photographs, but all correspondence is **subject to inspection by prison authorities** for security reasons. Letters may be opened and checked before being delivered, and items such as unauthorized documents, money, or small objects hidden in envelopes are prohibited. There is generally no limit on the number of letters inmates can send or receive, although restrictions may be applied if communication is considered a security concern.

Inmates are **not allowed to possess personal cell phones.** Instead, they may make phone calls through the prison's official telephone system. Calls are typically limited to a set duration, often around 10 minutes, and the number of calls permitted per week can vary depending on the facility's regulations. Inmates must provide an approved list of phone numbers—usually family or legal representatives—which must be pre-registered with the prison. Calls are monitored, and conversations deemed a security risk can be interrupted.

Visitation rules in Turkish prisons are relatively structured. Generally, inmates are entitled to **one open family visit per month** and **one closed visit per week**, though the frequency and length may vary by facility. Closed visits take place across a glass partition or using telephones, while open visits allow physical contact and longer interaction, usually with immediate family members. Special visits may be granted during national or religious holidays. Visitors must present valid identification, register in advance, and comply with strict security checks. Items such as electronic devices, food, or large bags are not permitted inside visiting areas.

As in many countries, the **exact rules may differ by prison**, so families should confirm visitation schedules, phone access, and mail procedures directly with the institution.

Prison Scams

Scams targeting families of incarcerated individuals in Turkey frequently exploit emotional vulnerabilities and confusion amid limited official communication. Common schemes include **impersonators posing as prisoners or prison officials** demanding urgent money for fictitious needs—such as medical treatment, legal fees, or commissary shortages. Some scammers masquerade as **lawyers offering sentence reductions** or early release for upfront payments. Others claim there's a special package awaiting the prisoner, requesting a **"delivery fee" or bribe for better treatment or more visitation time. Phishing attempts** via email or social media are also employed, with fraudsters pretending to be the inmate, their family, or legal contacts requesting money for mail clearance, commissary top-up, or call credits. A key red flag is urgent messaging with coerced secrecy, especially when accompanied by unusual payment methods like cryptocurrency, gift cards, or wire transfers. Discrepancies between the scammer's claims and known facts about prison rules, location, or inmate case status also indicate fraud.

If you suspect a scam, the first step is to **stop communication immediately** and verify the claim with the prison administration or via trusted legal contacts. You can report such scams or fraud attempts to the **Turkish National Police's Cyber Crimes Unit**, either in person or through a formal criminal complaint, as this is the official investigative body for these offenses. In parallel, it's possible to contact the **Chief Public Prosecutor's Office**, which oversees legal investigations. If funds were transferred, contact your bank without delay to attempt blocking the transaction; in some cases, judicial authorities may secure the suspect's account during legal proceedings.

Additionally, victims can reach out to the U.S. Embassy or Consulates in Turkey, which offer guidance on identifying and reporting fraud through their **Fraud Prevention Unit**. Raising awareness among family, friends, and support networks about these schemes is also crucial—education and vigilance are among the best defenses against falling victim.

Upon Release

In Turkey, foreigners released from prison or jail are often subject to **immigration-related procedures** in addition to completing their criminal sentence. Depending on the circumstances, they may be transferred directly to an **immigration removal center** for deportation proceedings, particularly if they no longer hold valid residency status or are considered a security risk. In some cases, foreigners may also be issued an **entry ban** preventing them from re-entering Turkey for a specified period.

Additional legal obligations after release depend on the case. Individuals on parole or serving a suspended sentence may be required to **report regularly to authorities**, comply with movement restrictions, or participate in supervision programs. For serious offenses, restrictions such as travel bans may remain in place until the sentence is fully cleared. Foreign nationals should also be aware that unresolved legal matters—such as pending appeals, fines, or civil claims—can affect their ability to leave the country even after release from prison.

CHAPTER 13

THE ADMINISTRATION OF JUSTICE

IN THIS CHAPTER

- Turkey's Legal System
- General Questions
- Law of the Land True Story
- Takeaways

CHAPTER 13

THE ADMINISTRATION OF JUSTICE

Turkey's Legal System

Turkey's legal system is rooted in the **civil law tradition**, with its foundations dating back to Atatürk's sweeping reforms in the 1920s. These reforms abolished Sharia courts and replaced the Ottoman millet-based religious system with a secular and codified structure. In 1926, Turkey adopted the **Swiss Civil Code**, while drawing on German commercial law and Italian criminal law, establishing a comprehensive framework that continues to underpin its modern legal system. At the center of this system stands the **Constitution of Turkey**, which is the supreme law of the land and provides the foundation for civil, penal, administrative, and commercial codes. As in other civil law jurisdictions, judicial decisions are based primarily on codified statutes rather than precedent.

The judiciary is organized in a hierarchical structure with several high courts at the top. The **Constitutional Court** reviews the constitutionality of laws and government actions, while also hearing individual applications for violations of fundamental rights. The **Court of Cassation** functions as the highest appellate court for civil and criminal cases, and the **Council of State** serves as the top administrative court, resolving disputes involving public authorities, taxation, and government employment. Other specialized bodies include the **Court of Jurisdictional Disputes**, which resolves conflicts between judicial authorities, and the **Court of Accounts**, which is responsible for auditing public finances.

Beneath these high courts, **civil courts** oversee matters such as family law, commercial disputes, and property cases, while criminal courts handle offenses ranging from misdemeanors to serious crimes depending on their level. **Administrative courts**, meanwhile, focus on challenges to government actions and regulations.

Distinctive features of the Turkish judiciary include its strong reliance on codified law, the division of judicial authority among several specialized high courts, and the centralized role of the Ministry of Justice and the Council of Judges and Prosecutors in judicial administration. While these structures are designed to ensure order and consistency, they have also been subject to criticism regarding independence and impartiality. Since the 2016 coup attempt, in particular, concerns about political interference have grown as thousands of judges and prosecutors were dismissed and replaced, often with individuals seen as loyal to the government (see *Law of the Land True Story* below).

The main challenges facing Turkey's judiciary today include **backlogs** in the courts, **uneven application of justice**, and most significantly, **threats to judicial independence.** International bodies such as the Council of Europe, along with human rights groups, have raised alarms about the politicization of judicial appointments, erosion of fair trial protections, and the use of the legal system to target journalists, political opposition figures, and civil society organizations. These challenges highlight broader issues within Turkey's democratic system, particularly the dominance of the executive branch over other institutions and the weakening of checks and balances. Concerns about corruption, lack of transparency, and executive pressure on the courts continue to fuel debate over the state of rule of law in the country.

General Questions

1. ***Will the court treat first-time offenders and tourists with more leniency?*** In Turkey, courts consider a defendant's background, criminal history, and the circumstances of the offense. First-time offenders may receive reduced or suspended sentences for minor crimes, but **leniency is not guaranteed** and depends on the crime and any mitigating factors. Foreign tourists are subject to the same laws as Turkish citizens. Being a tourist does not automatically lead to leniency, though minor, unintentional offenses may be viewed more gently. Ignorance of the law is not a defense, and serious crimes—such as drug offenses, violence, or threats to national security—are punished just as strictly for foreigners as for citizens.

2. ***If I am charged with a crime, which court is likely to hear my case?*** In Turkey, the court that hears your case depends on the nature and seriousness of the crime. Minor offenses are heard by Criminal Peace Courts, crimes with potential sentences up to 10 years go to Criminal Courts of First Instance, and the most serious crimes, like homicide or drug trafficking, are tried in Heavy Criminal Courts. Juvenile Courts handle offenders under 18. There are no juries; judges decide cases, which can be appealed to Regional Courts of Appeal, and the highest review for legal errors is the Court of Cassation.

3. ***What is the standard of proof in a criminal case in Turkey?*** In Turkey, the standard of proof in a criminal case is **"beyond a reasonable doubt."** The prosecution must present sufficient evidence to convince the judge that the accused committed the crime. If there is any reasonable doubt about the defendant's guilt, the court is required to acquit.

Law of the Land True Story[16]

The 2016 coup attempt in Turkey occurred on July 15, when a faction of the military tried to overthrow President Erdoğan's government. The coup plotters claimed they were acting to restore democracy, alleging that the government had become increasingly authoritarian. Military units seized key locations in Ankara and Istanbul, including bridges, airports, and state television stations, and attempted to detain senior officials. Fighting broke out between coup forces and loyalist military, police, and civilians, resulting in over 300 deaths and more than 2,000 injuries. Civilians resisted, confronting soldiers and tanks, and the coup collapsed within about 12 hours.

Afterward, the government declared a state of emergency and launched a massive purge across the military, judiciary, civil service, education, and media, targeting individuals accused of links to the Gülen movement, which the government held responsible for the coup. Tens of thousands of people were arrested, dismissed, or suspended from their positions. Critics argue that these purges undermined judicial independence, centralized power under the executive, and raised concerns about human rights and political freedoms. The coup reflected deep political polarization, tensions between secularists and the increasingly conservative government, and rivalries within the military.

Specifically for the judiciary, thousands of judges and prosecutors were dismissed and replaced, often with individuals seen as loyal to the government. This restructuring increased executive influence over the courts, weakening judicial independence and raising concerns about impartiality and fair trial protections in Turkey.

16 https://www.washingtonpost.com/world/turkeys-suspension-of-thousands-of-judges-marked-the-start-of-a-widespread-purge/2016/07/20/dbf79e18-4c50-11e6-bf27-405106836f96_story.html

Takeaways

Turkey's legal system is based on civil law, rooted in Atatürk's 1920s reforms, with codified statutes from the Swiss Civil Code, German commercial law, and Italian criminal law forming the basis for modern law.

The judiciary is hierarchical, with high courts such as the Constitutional Court, Court of Cassation, and Council of State at the top, followed by specialized, civil, criminal, and administrative courts. Judges make decisions without juries.

Courts consider the defendant's background, criminal history, and circumstances. Minor offenses may result in leniency for first-time offenders, but serious crimes are punished equally for citizens and foreigners. Criminal cases are heard in courts appropriate to the crime's severity, and the standard of proof is "beyond a reasonable doubt."

The judiciary faces issues such as political influence, executive dominance, backlogs, and uneven application of justice, raising concerns about fair trial protections and rule of law.

CHAPTER 14

CRIME VICTIM ASSISTANCE

IN THIS CHAPTER

- Overview
- What to Do If You Are the Victim of a Crime
- Common Tourist Scams in Turkey
- Consular Assistance
- General Questions

CHAPTER 14

CRIME VICTIM ASSISTANCE

Overview

Crime victims in Turkey have access to a variety of resources through both government services and non-governmental organizations. The Turkish government provides **Victim Support Centers** (**Mağdur Destek Merkezleri**) in many cities, offering legal guidance, psychological counseling, and assistance navigating the judicial process. These services are confidential and available to all victims, including foreigners and tourists. Information about the nearest center can be found on the Ministry of Justice website at **www.adalet.gov.tr.**

Non-governmental organizations also play an important role in supporting victims. For example, **Mor Çatı** supports women experiencing domestic violence, **Türkiye Çocuklara Yeniden Özgürlük Vakfı** (**Turkey Foundation for Children's Freedom**) helps child victims, and the **Turkish Red Crescent** (**Kızılay**) provides emergency shelter, counseling, and other aid to vulnerable populations.

Emergency assistance in Turkey is accessible via the **national emergency number 112**, which connects callers to police, medical, and fire services. For gender-based violence, victims can contact the **183 Social Support Line**, offering confidential support and guidance. These resources ensure that victims can access timely help and protection throughout the country.

What to Do If You Are the Victim of a Crime

If you become a victim of a crime in Turkey, your first priority is your safety. Call **112**, the national emergency number, for immediate assistance from police, medical services, or fire authorities. If the situation is not an emergency but still serious, go to the nearest police station (Emniyet Müdürlüğü or Jandarma) to file a **formal complaint** (**şikayet**), which is necessary to start an official investigation. If you do not speak Turkish, you can request an interpreter.

For victims of sexual assault, it is especially important to seek medical attention immediately, even if there are no visible injuries. Hospitals can provide treatment, collect forensic evidence, and document your condition. If possible, avoid cleaning or disturbing the scene of the assault, as evidence may be crucial. You can request a female doctor or nurse if that makes you more comfortable.

After reporting the crime, you can contact a **Victim Support Center** (**Mağdur Destek Merkezi**) for free legal guidance, psychological support, and assistance navigating the judicial process. These services are available to all victims, including foreigners. NGOs such as Mor Çatı, Türkiye Çocuklara Yeniden Özgürlük Vakfı, and the Turkish Red Crescent can also provide specialized help depending on the type of crime, including sexual violence, domestic abuse, or trafficking.

Keep all documentation, including the police report, medical records, forensic reports, and any correspondence with authorities, as these may be needed for legal proceedings or insurance purposes. If your passport or ID was stolen, contact your embassy or consulate immediately to arrange replacements. Throughout the process, prioritize your safety and confidentiality.

Common Tourist Scams in Turkey

Tourists in Turkey are often targeted by a variety of scams, especially in busy cities like Istanbul, Antalya, and tourist-heavy areas like the Grand Bazaar or beach resorts. Common scams include **pickpocketing** in crowded markets, public transport, and tourist sites, often carried out by groups using distractions, such as someone bumping into you or dropping something near you while an accomplice steals your belongings.

Other frequent scams involve **unofficial guides** offering tours or help at ticket counters, ATMs, or transportation hubs, then demanding excessive tips or attempting to steal your card information. The **"friendship bracelet"** trick is also seen, where someone places a bracelet on your wrist and insists on payment. Tourists may also encounter **fake police officers** who ask to inspect your wallet or passport under the pretense of checking for counterfeit money.

To avoid these scams, stay alert in crowded areas, keep valuables secure and out of sight, and be cautious of unsolicited help or overly friendly strangers. Never hand over your wallet or personal documents to someone claiming to be an official—ask for proper identification and, if unsure, go to the nearest police station. **Trust your instincts:** persistent or suspicious behavior is often a warning sign.

Consular Assistance

If you become a victim of a crime in Turkey, your embassy or consulate can provide several types of support. As mentioned throughout various chapters in the book, they can offer guidance on local laws and the judicial process, help you locate a lawyer, and provide information on Victim Support Centers or NGOs that offer legal, medical, or psychological assistance. Consular staff can also contact your family or friends on your behalf and help replace stolen or lost passports and travel documents.

However, consular assistance has limitations. Embassies and consulates cannot intervene in the legal process, provide direct financial assistance, or act as your legal representative in court. They also cannot influence the outcome of criminal investigations or guarantee special treatment from local authorities. Their role is primarily to provide **guidance, resources, and logistical support** to help you navigate the situation safely.

General Questions

1. ***If I am a victim of a crime, can I legally be compensated?*** **Yes.** Victims of crime in Turkey can seek legal compensation, depending on the nature of the offense and the outcome of criminal or civil proceedings. Victims may request restitution from the offender to cover medical expenses, property damage, lost income, or emotional distress. Compensation can be pursued either through the criminal trial, where the court may order the offender to pay damages, or via a separate civil lawsuit. In some cases, the government provides limited financial support for victims of violent crimes if the offender cannot pay, though these programs are restricted. Promptly reporting the crime, keeping thorough documentation, and consulting a lawyer or a Victim Support Center are essential steps for pursuing compensation.

2. ***If a family member falls victim to homicide, can I bring the body back to my home country?*** **Yes.** If a family member is the victim of homicide in Turkey, you can repatriate the body to your home country, but the process involves several legal and administrative steps. Turkish authorities must first complete the criminal investigation and issue a death certificate. The body may also need a post-mortem or forensic examination, especially in cases of suspicious or violent death. You will need to work with your embassy or consulate, a local funeral home or mortuary, and possibly a licensed transportation company that handles international repatriation. Required documents typically include the death certificate, a consular mortuary certificate, and permits for transport. Regulations and procedures can vary depending on the country of origin, so early coordination with consular officials is crucial to ensure compliance with both Turkish and home-country requirements.

3. ***If a family member falls victim to homicide, will I receive any assistance from the Turkish government?*** **Yes.** If a family member is the victim of homicide in Turkey, you may receive **limited assistance** from the Turkish authorities. Law enforcement and local officials will help guide you through the investigative and legal process, including providing information about the case, facilitating access to the body, and coordinating with the embassy or consulate for repatriation. Victim Support Centers can also offer emotional support, guidance on legal rights, and assistance with navigating the judicial system. However, the Turkish government does not provide financial compensation directly to family members, and any support is primarily administrative, logistical, or advisory.

CHAPTER 15

POLICE

IN THIS CHAPTER

- Overview
- Police Response and Community Relations
- Police Use of Force
- Law of the Land True Story

CHAPTER 15
POLICE

Overview[17]

Turkey's law enforcement system is structured across multiple levels, encompassing national, regional, and local agencies, each with distinct responsibilities. The system is designed to cover urban centers, rural areas, and specialized security needs, while maintaining coordination between civil and paramilitary branches. The police work closely with prosecutors and the judiciary to enforce laws, investigate crimes, and ensure public order. Additionally, Turkey has specialized units within its police forces for counter-terrorism, organized crime, cybercrime, and VIP protection, reflecting the country's diverse security challenges.

At the national level, the **General Directorate of Security (Emniyet Genel Müdürlüğü)** serves as the primary civilian police force. It is responsible for urban law enforcement, traffic control, counter-terrorism, and the protection of VIPs and foreign diplomats. The Directorate operates under the Ministry of the Interior and is organized into 81 provincial directorates and 751 district directorates, ensuring coverage across all regions of Turkey. Urban policing also includes specialized units such as the Anti-Smuggling and Organized Crime Department (KOM), the Counter-Terrorism Unit, and Cybercrime units, which address specific threats within cities.

17 https://en.wikipedia.org/wiki/Law_enforcement_in_Turkey

The **Gendarmerie General Command** (**Jandarma Genel Komutanlığı**) functions as a paramilitary force under the Ministry of the Interior, focusing primarily on rural law enforcement, border security, and maintaining public order outside urban centers. The Gendarmerie has a dual role: acting as a military-style organization for internal security while also performing civilian policing duties in villages and smaller towns. It comprises close to 200,000 active personnel and operates checkpoints, border patrols, and anti-smuggling operations. The Gendarmerie also supports counter-terrorism operations in regions with higher security risks, often in collaboration with the Turkish National Police.

Municipal police forces, known as **Belediye zabıtası**, operate at the local level, enforcing city ordinances, traffic rules, public safety regulations, and municipal code compliance. Their authority is limited compared to the National Police or Gendarmerie—they do not investigate serious criminal offenses but are responsible for managing day-to-day public order in neighborhoods, markets, and city centers. Municipal police also support community policing initiatives and local civil protection measures, such as enforcing building safety regulations, noise ordinances, and local business compliance.

As of 2024, the **Turkish National Police** (**TNP**) employs over 350,000 personnel, making it one of the largest civilian employers in the country. When combined with the Gendarmerie and other specialized forces, the total number of law enforcement personnel in Turkey reaches around 420,000 personnel, which equates to roughly **one officer per 163 inhabitants.** This staffing level is significant compared to many countries; however, challenges remain, particularly in rural or remote regions where coverage can be limited and crime patterns differ. These challenges sometimes require rapid redeployment of personnel or reliance on specialized units for specific incidents.[18]

While Turkey maintains a substantial law enforcement presence, concerns have been raised about **uneven distribution of personnel**, particularly in rural areas where the Gendarmerie is the primary policing authority. Staffing adequacy can be affected by regional security threats,

18 https://sk.sagepub.com/ency/edvol/lawenforcement/chpt/turkey

counter-terrorism needs, large-scale public events, or seasonal tourism surges. Urban centers generally have well-staffed and technologically equipped police units, while smaller towns and border regions may experience delays in response or limited access to specialized investigative capabilities. Despite these challenges, Turkey's police system remains highly centralized, with structured hierarchies and coordination mechanisms intended to maintain public safety across the country.

Police Response and Community Relations

Turkey's police force is generally viewed as **highly organized and centralized**, which allows for relatively rapid responses in urban areas, particularly major cities like Istanbul, Ankara, and Izmir. Emergency calls to the national police number, **155**, typically connect citizens to local units, and incidents involving serious crimes, accidents, or public disturbances are usually prioritized. Specialized units within the Turkish National Police, such as the Counter-Terrorism, Organized Crime, and Cybercrime divisions, are deployed for incidents that require expert handling, which adds to operational efficiency in complex cases.

In urban centers, response times are often adequate, especially in areas with heavy police presence or advanced surveillance systems. Traffic accidents, thefts, and minor disturbances are generally addressed quickly, although some delays may occur in high-density districts or during peak times. In contrast, **rural and remote areas** rely heavily on the Gendarmerie, where response times can be longer due to geographic challenges, limited staffing, and fewer technological resources.

Domestically, the Turkish police enjoy a **mixed reputation**. Many citizens trust the force to maintain public order and respond to emergencies efficiently. However, concerns have been raised about **political influence, corruption, and selective enforcement**, particularly after the above discussed coup attempt when mass purges affected thousands of officers. These issues have led to skepticism about impartiality in politically sensitive cases, although day-to-day policing for ordinary citizens remains generally reliable.

Internationally, perceptions of the Turkish police are also mixed. Tourism authorities and expatriate communities often praise the **visibility of police presence in tourist areas** and the generally effective handling of routine crimes. At the same time, human rights organizations and foreign observers have criticized certain aspects of law enforcement, including **alleged excessive use of force during protests, politically motivated investigations, and restrictions on press freedom**, which can affect the international image of the police force.

Police Use of Force[19]

Police use of force in Turkey is considered a **significant concern.** Both domestic and international human rights organizations, including Amnesty International and the International Federation for Human Rights (FIDH), have documented repeated instances of excessive or disproportionate force, particularly against peaceful protesters, political demonstrators, and minority groups. Reports highlight the use of tear gas, water cannons, rubber and plastic bullets, pepper spray, and batons, often in ways that cause serious injuries or target individuals who are not posing a threat.

High-profile incidents, such as the **May Day 2024 protests in Istanbul** and the **March 2025 demonstrations following the detention of Istanbul Mayor Ekrem İmamoğlu**, exemplify these concerns. (See *Law of the Land True Story* below.) In both cases, law enforcement employed large numbers of officers and heavy-handed tactics to disperse crowds, resulting in widespread criticism from human rights groups and international observers.

The ongoing pattern of **excessive force, lack of accountability, and reported intimidation of victims** underscores why police conduct is a major concern in Turkey. Reforms and investigations have been limited, and critics argue that systemic changes are needed to ensure proper oversight and protection of civil rights.

19 https://www.independent.co.uk/news/ekrem-imamoglu-istanbul-turkey-recep-tayyip-erdogan-b2735667.html

Law of the Land True Story[20]

On March 19, 2025, Istanbul Mayor Ekrem İmamoğlu, a prominent opposition figure and potential presidential candidate, was arrested by Turkish authorities on charges including corruption and alleged links to terrorism. His detention, viewed by many as politically motivated, prompted widespread protests across Turkey. The demonstrations were met with a heavy-handed response from law enforcement. In Istanbul, Ankara, and other cities, riot police deployed tear gas, pepper spray, and water cannons to disperse crowds. At least 1,900 individuals were detained during the unrest, including protesters and journalists covering the events.

The crackdown also extended to the media. At least 11 local journalists were detained in Istanbul and Izmir for their reporting on the protests. Seven of them were remanded in detention on charges related to violating laws on meetings and demonstrations, though they were later released pending trial. This suppression of press freedom further underscores the challenges to democratic norms in the country.

20 https://www.independent.co.uk/news/ekrem-imamoglu-istanbul-turkey-recep-tayyip-erdogan-b2735667.html

CHAPTER 16

HOW TO GET LEGAL HELP IN TURKEY

IN THIS CHAPTER

- Available Resources
- Legal Aid
- Foreign Embassies in Turkey

CHAPTER 16

HOW TO GET LEGAL HELP IN TURKEY

Available Resources

If you are arrested or require legal help in Turkey, it is essential to know where to turn for reliable support. Turkish law guarantees your right to legal representation, and you may contact a lawyer immediately. If you cannot afford a lawyer, you are entitled to a **public defender**, known locally as an *adli yardım avukatı*.

To secure trustworthy legal representation, you can request a list of local attorneys from the police or contact **the Union of Turkish Bar Associations** (***Türkiye Barolar Birliği***), which provides referrals to qualified lawyers. Many attorneys in Turkey speak English or other foreign languages, making it possible to communicate effectively in your preferred language.

Embassies and consulates are important points of support for foreigners. They often maintain lists of local lawyers who speak your language and understand the Turkish legal system. These lists are typically available on the consulate's website. It is advisable to contact your embassy or consulate as soon as possible after an arrest. They can provide guidance, assist with communication, and help you navigate the legal process in Turkey.

In addition, organizations such as the **International Red Cross** and **local non-governmental organizations** provide assistance to individuals facing legal difficulties, including victims of crime or those in detention. These organizations can offer support, translation services, and referrals to legal professionals. Local **legal aid services** (Adli Yardım) are also available for eligible individuals.

For further information, the Union of Turkish Bar Associations can be accessed at **www.barobirlik.org.tr**, and the Turkish Red Cross can be reached through **www.kizilay.org.tr**.

Legal Aid

Foreign visitors in Turkey may be eligible for legal aid if they meet **specific criteria.** Legal aid is available to both Turkish citizens and foreigners, including non-EU nationals, provided they can demonstrate **insufficient financial resources** to cover the costs of legal representation. This support extends to criminal, civil, administrative, and labor law proceedings, as well as to individuals who are victims of certain crimes, including domestic violence, human trafficking, or terrorism-related offenses. Legal aid ensures that those who cannot afford legal representation still have access to justice and are able to participate fully in legal proceedings.

To apply for legal aid, applicants should **contact the local Bar Association** (Baro) in the city where their case is being handled. Many Bar Associations operate a dedicated Legal Aid Service that guides applicants through the process. Applicants must provide documentation such as proof of identity, evidence of income and assets, and any relevant legal case documents. A commission within the Bar Association reviews the application and determines eligibility based on financial need and the nature of the legal matter. Certain groups, such as victims of domestic violence, may be granted legal aid automatically without a detailed financial assessment, ensuring urgent support is provided where it is most needed.

Eligibility for legal aid is primarily **determined by financial circumstances.** Applicants must show that they cannot afford legal representation, with factors such as monthly income, household composition, and outstanding financial obligations taken into consideration. Once approved, legal aid in Turkey can include initial legal advice, full representation by a lawyer, coverage of court fees, and costs related to expert witnesses or reports. In some cases, it may also cover certain administrative fees required for official documentation or certifications, allowing applicants to navigate the legal system without incurring prohibitive costs.

For further guidance, the Union of Turkish Bar Associations provides information and support regarding legal aid and can be accessed at www.barobirlik.org.tr. Bar Associations remain the primary point of contact for applicants, offering advice, assistance, and referrals to eligible legal aid services.

Foreign Embassies in Turkey

Embassies and consulates serve distinct yet complementary roles in international diplomacy. **Embassies**, typically located in a nation's capital, are led by ambassadors and handle high-level diplomatic relations, policy discussions, and representation of their home country's interests to the host government. **Consulates**, in contrast, are generally located in major cities outside the capital and focus on providing services to citizens abroad, including issuing passports, assisting in emergencies, facilitating trade, and promoting cultural exchanges. Together, these missions form the backbone of a country's diplomatic presence, supporting both government-to-government relations and citizen services.

As of 2025, Turkey hosts over **120 resident embassies**, all situated in **Ankara**, the nation's political center. In addition, there are numerous **consular offices** throughout the country, including official consulates-general and honorary consulates, distributed across major cities such as **Istanbul, Izmir, Antalya, and Adana**. These consular offices provide essential services to both foreign nationals and Turkish citizens, from visa processing and travel documentation to emergency assistance and the promotion of trade and cultural programs. The network of embassies and consulates ensures that diplomatic, economic, and cultural relations are maintained effectively across the country.

Prominent embassies in Ankara include those of the **United States, United Kingdom, Germany, France, China, and Russia**, all of which play key roles in fostering diplomatic relations, trade negotiations, and cultural exchange. The United States, for example, maintains a robust diplomatic presence in Turkey, with its embassy in **Ankara** and consulates in **Istanbul, Adana, and Izmir**. These missions provide a wide range of services, including visa processing, support for U.S. citizens, and initiatives to strengthen bilateral relations, business ties, and educational programs.

ADDITIONAL INFORMATION

For a comprehensive list of foreign embassies and consulates in Turkey, you can refer to the official directory of the Turkish Ministry of Foreign Affairs at **www.mfa.gov.tr**. Additionally, the U.S. Department of State offers information on U.S. embassies and consulates worldwide at **www.usembassy.gov**.

CHAPTER 17

MEDICAL FACILITIES & HOSPITALS

IN THIS CHAPTER

- Overview
- Visitors' Access to Healthcare in Turkey
- Hospitals in Turkey
- Insurance Guidance
- General Questions

CHAPTER 17

MEDICAL FACILITIES & HOSPITALS

Overview

Turkey's healthcare system has undergone significant reforms over the past two decades and is now considered **one of the most rapidly developing healthcare systems** among OECD countries. The system is built on a mix of **public and private healthcare services**, with the public sector forming the backbone of medical care. Public healthcare is primarily managed by the Ministry of Health under the **General Health Insurance** (**Genel Sağlık Sigortası – GSS**) scheme, which provides coverage for Turkish citizens and legal residents. Funded through taxation and social security contributions, the public system includes access to general practitioners, hospital care, specialist treatment, maternity services, and emergency care.

Healthcare in Turkey operates through a network of **state hospitals, university hospitals, and family health centers**, complemented by private hospitals and clinics. The **public system** provides **affordable and often free services** to those covered under GSS, while the **private sector** offers faster access to specialists, shorter waiting times, and luxury facilities, often attracting both locals with private insurance and medical tourists. Many residents choose to supplement public coverage with **private health insurance**, which is **relatively affordable** compared to Western Europe and allows for greater choice of doctors and hospitals.

In terms of accessibility, healthcare services are widely available across Turkey, with hospitals and clinics found in nearly every province. Major cities such as Istanbul, Ankara, and Izmir boast modern, internationally accredited hospitals equipped with advanced medical technology, while rural areas may have fewer facilities but still benefit from the nationwide network of family health centers. The **quality of care** is considered **high,** especially in urban centers and private hospitals, many of which cater to international patients.

Turkey is also a **hub for medical tourism**, particularly in fields such as cosmetic surgery, dentistry, fertility treatments, and cardiology, due to its combination of skilled professionals and competitive prices.

Affordability is a key strength of Turkey's healthcare system. For residents covered under GSS, public healthcare is low-cost or free at the point of use, with only minimal co-payments for certain services or prescription medications. Private healthcare, while more expensive, is still more affordable than in many European or North American countries, making it an attractive option for both locals and foreigners seeking prompt, specialized care.

Visitors' Access to Healthcare in Turkey

Visitors to Turkey have access to both **public and private healthcare services**, but the way they receive and pay for treatment depends largely on their **insurance coverage** and residency status. Unlike Turkish citizens and legal residents covered by the national **General Health Insurance** (**GSS**) scheme, tourists and short-term visitors are not automatically entitled to subsidized healthcare. Instead, they typically rely on **travel health insurance** purchased before arrival or pay **out-of-pocket** at the point of care. For those with travel insurance, most private hospitals and some public hospitals will accept coverage, though in many cases visitors may need to pay first and later seek reimbursement from their insurance provider.

In terms of cost, **private hospitals** are generally the preferred option for visitors, as they often provide quicker service, English-speaking staff, and internationally accredited facilities. Out-of-pocket costs at private hospitals are significantly lower than in many Western countries but can still vary depending on the type of treatment or emergency. In contrast, **public hospitals** are cheaper, but visitors without insurance will be required to pay the full cost, and language support may be limited. To ensure peace of mind, most travelers are strongly advised to have **comprehensive travel health insurance** that covers emergencies, hospitalization, and, if needed, medical evacuation.

Language barriers can sometimes present challenges for visitors seeking medical help, particularly in rural areas or smaller towns where English proficiency may be limited. However, in larger cities, as well as in popular tourist regions, many doctors and healthcare staff in private hospitals speak English, German, Russian, or Arabic, reflecting Turkey's international visitor base. In fact, Turkey's **growing medical tourism industry** means that many hospitals have dedicated international patient units with multilingual staff to assist foreign patients with registration, translation, billing, and insurance procedures.

For emergencies, visitors can call **112**, Turkey's nationwide emergency number, which provides **ambulance, police, and fire services.** Operators may not always speak fluent English, but multilingual support is common. Visitors can also contact their hotel, embassy, or travel insurance provider for assistance in navigating the healthcare system, finding English-speaking doctors, or arranging appointments. **Pharmacies** (**eczane**) are also widely available and are often the first point of contact for minor illnesses; pharmacists are highly trained and may be able to provide basic medical advice and over-the-counter medications.

Overall, visitors to Turkey can expect **high-quality medical care**, particularly in private facilities, with costs that are affordable by international standards. With adequate travel health insurance, access to healthcare is straightforward, and in major tourist and urban areas, language barriers are increasingly being addressed through international patient services and multilingual staff.

Hospitals in Turkey

Turkey has a vast and growing healthcare infrastructure supported by both public and private sectors. According to available data, the country had more than 30,000 health institutions in the last decade, with an average of **one doctor per 573 patients** and about **2.6 hospital beds per 1,000 people.**[21] As of 2025, there are at least 269 government hospitals across the country, with Istanbul alone accounting for 43 of them, making it the single province with the highest concentration.[22] In addition to state hospitals, Turkey has a robust private healthcare sector, with major groups such as **Acıbadem Healthcare Group**, which operates 29 hospitals and 15 medical centers with nearly 29,000 staff, and Medical Park, which runs 17 hospitals with more than 6,000 doctors and staff.

Hospitals in Turkey are most **heavily concentrated in large metropolitan areas** such as **Istanbul, Ankara, and Izmir**, which serve as the country's primary hubs of advanced medical care. Other cities with significant hospital infrastructure include **Antalya, Adana, and Konya**. These centers are not only home to state hospitals but also to many of the country's top private institutions, which attract international patients due to their advanced facilities and multilingual services.

Among the best-known hospitals in Turkey are the **Acıbadem hospitals**, which are JCI-accredited and internationally recognized for oncology, cardiology, organ transplants, and robotic surgery, and the **Anadolu Medical Center** in Gebze, which is affiliated with Johns Hopkins Medicine and specializes in cancer care, neurosurgery, and transplants. **Memorial Hospitals**, particularly in Istanbul's Şişli district, are also highly regarded for cardiology, oncology, and robotic surgery, while **Liv Hospital** in Ulus is known for advanced technology and minimally invasive procedures. **Medipol Mega University Hospital** in Istanbul is one of the largest private university hospitals in the country, excelling in neurosurgery and cardiovascular care, while **Koç University Hospital** is respected for its research-oriented approach and excellence in oncology and transplantation. **Florence Nightingale Hospital**, which pioneered

21 https://en.wikipedia.org/wiki/Health_in_Turkey

22 https://www.poidata.io/report/government-hospital/turkey/

private heart surgery in Turkey, continues to have a strong reputation in cardiovascular and transplant medicine.

For international visitors, Turkey offers many hospitals that cater specifically to foreign patients with multilingual staff and international patient departments. Facilities such as Acıbadem, Anadolu, Memorial, Liv, Medipol, and Koç University Hospital all have dedicated units to assist with interpretation, insurance, and travel logistics. These services make Turkey one of the leading global destinations for medical tourism, especially in specialties such as oncology, cardiology, fertility, cosmetic surgery, and organ transplants.

There is also a long-standing American institution in Istanbul: **the Vehbi Koç Foundation American Hospital.** Originally founded in 1920, it is a private, non-profit general hospital located in the city's Nişantaşı district. Today it has nearly 300 beds, modern surgical units, and internationally accredited facilities. The American Hospital is highly regarded for its quality of care and comprehensive services, and remains a popular choice for both locals and international visitors.

In summary, Turkey's hospital system is diverse, with a strong public foundation complemented by a rapidly growing private sector that meets international standards. With thousands of doctors, internationally accredited facilities, and a concentration of top-tier hospitals in major cities, Turkey not only provides essential healthcare to its citizens but also serves as a global hub for international patients seeking affordable, high-quality medical care.

Insurance Guidance

Foreign insurance plans are generally accepted in Turkey, but **mainly at private hospitals and clinics.** Public hospitals usually do not bill foreign insurance directly, so visitors without local coverage must pay **out-of-pocket** and later submit claims to their insurance provider. Travelers from outside the EU or Turkey—such as those from the U.S., Canada, or Australia—should carry **proof of private travel insurance** that covers international care and confirm with their provider which hospitals or clinics are partnered with their plan. Checking this in advance can help avoid unexpected costs and ensure faster service.

Medical costs in Turkey are generally lower than in many Western countries, though they vary between public and private facilities. For example, **non-emergency doctor's visit** in a private clinic typically costs **₺200–500 (roughly $10–25 USD)**, while an **emergency room visit** may range from **₺500–1,500** (**about $25–75 USD**) depending on the severity of the issue and any tests performed. Hospitalization, surgeries, or advanced diagnostic procedures can be more expensive, though they usually remain more affordable than similar care in North America or Western Europe.

Most travelers pay **directly at the time of treatment**, using cash or credit/debit card. It is important to request a detailed receipt and, if relevant, a medical report to submit to your insurance provider for reimbursement. Some high-end private hospitals may offer **direct billing** for international insurance plans with known providers, but it is recommended to confirm this before your visit. Keeping your insurance policy number, emergency contacts, and a summary of coverage on hand can make the process smoother and reduce delays in receiving care.

General Questions

1. ***What number do I call in a medical emergency?*** Dial **112**, Turkey's nationwide emergency number, for immediate access to ambulance, police, or fire services. You can call from any phone, and in major cities, operators can assist in English, though proficiency may be limited in rural areas.

2. ***Will I be treated if I don't have insurance?*** **Yes. Emergency medical care is provided to everyone**, regardless of insurance status or nationality. However, you will likely need to pay for services upfront if you do not have travel insurance, and you can later submit receipts to your insurer for reimbursement.

3. ***Can I find English-speaking doctors in Turkey?*** **Yes.** English-speaking doctors are **widely available in major cities and private hospitals**, as well as in tourist areas. Some public hospitals in large cities also have English-speaking staff or interpreters. In smaller towns, a translation app or basic Turkish phrasebook may be helpful.

4. ***Should I go to a public or private hospital?*** It depends. Public hospitals provide reliable emergency care and are well-equipped in urban areas, but wait times can be long and English may not be widely spoken. Private hospitals typically have shorter wait times, more English-speaking staff, and better service for international patients. If your travel insurance covers private care, these facilities are often the most convenient option.

5. ***Do I need to pay upfront for medical treatment?*** In public hospitals, all visitors, including foreigners, usually must pay **out-of-pocket** for non-emergency services. Private hospitals almost always require payment at the time of treatment, though they may accept direct billing if your travel insurance has a local partner. Keeping receipts is essential for insurance reimbursement.

6. ***What if I need a prescription in Turkey?*** For most medications, you will need to see a local doctor to obtain a prescription. Once issued, prescriptions can be filled at any pharmacy (eczane). Many common medications are available over the counter, but for controlled or specialty drugs, a doctor's prescription is required.

7. ***Can I bring my medication to Turkey?*** **Yes.** Bring all medication in the **original packaging** along with a **prescription or doctor's note**, especially for controlled substances. Check Turkish customs rules if you are carrying large quantities or certain restricted medications.

CHAPTER 18

DRIVING IN TURKEY

IN THIS CHAPTER

- Overview
- Main Traffic Rules
- General Questions
- Law of the Land Hypothetical

CHAPTER 18
DRIVING IN TURKEY

Overview

Driving in Turkey is a mixed experience, balancing the ease of modern highways with the challenges of busy city streets and rural roads. In large cities, traffic can be heavy, drivers tend to be assertive, and congestion is common, especially during peak hours. Once outside the urban centers, the motorway network is generally modern, well-marked, and well-maintained, making long-distance travel relatively smooth. Rural and mountain roads can be narrower, winding, and less well-lit, and in some remote areas surfaces may be rougher, so extra caution is needed.

Foreign drivers can use their national license for **up to six months**, and while this applies to many countries, an **International Driving Permit is strongly recommended** and often required by rental companies. Insurance is compulsory, with rental cars including basic liability coverage and the option to add more comprehensive protection. Those driving their own car into Turkey must carry a Green Card insurance certificate that is valid in the country.

Driving habits in Turkey can take some adjustment. The country drives on the **right**, seatbelts are required for all passengers, and phones may only be used with hands-free systems. Headlights flashed from oncoming cars usually signal "I am coming through" rather than yielding, and roundabout etiquette is not always consistent, as some drivers push through regardless of the right of way. In rural areas, it is common to encounter tractors, animals, or pedestrians on the road, and in cities horns are used more frequently than many visitors may expect.

Most motorways and major bridges are **toll roads**, and Turkey uses a **cashless system** for payment. The main method is the **HGS electronic sticker**, which attaches to the windshield and automatically deducts tolls. Older OGS transponders are still in use but are being phased out. Rental cars are generally equipped with an HGS tag, and charges are added to the rental account, while foreign drivers in private cars must purchase and load credit onto an HGS sticker from post offices or participating fuel stations before entering toll roads.

Overall, driving in Turkey is very manageable for foreign visitors who are prepared for local habits, bring the right documents and insurance, and make sure they have arranged an HGS for toll payments. The combination of well-developed highways and scenic rural routes makes it an excellent way to explore the country.

Main Traffic Rules & Road Safety Tips

- **Driving side:** Vehicles drive on the **right-hand side** of the road, with overtaking on the left.
- **Speed limits:** Generally **50 km/h (31 mph)** in urban areas, **90 km/h (56 mph)** on rural roads, and **120 km/h (75 mph)** on highways, though signs should always be checked as limits can vary.
- **Traffic signals:** Standard international system of **red, yellow, and green lights** is used. Drivers may treat red lights more loosely than in some countries, so extra caution is advised at intersections.
- **Seat belts: Mandatory for all passengers**, both in the front and back seats.
- **Alcohol:** The legal blood alcohol limit is **0.05%.** For professional drivers and drivers of commercial vehicles, the limit is **0.00%.** Penalties for drink-driving are strict.

- **Mobile devices:** Use of mobile phones while driving is **prohibited** unless via a hands-free system.
- **Toll roads:** Most major highways and bridges are tolled. Payment is **electronic only via the HGS sticker** (or OGS in some older cases). Rental cars typically come with an HGS device.
- **If stopped by police:** Remain in the vehicle unless asked otherwise. Police may request to see your license, passport, car registration, and insurance papers. Random traffic checks are common, especially in rural areas.
- **Road safety:** Turkish highways are generally modern and safe, but driver behavior can be unpredictable. Accidents are more common in urban and rural areas due to aggressive driving styles, so vigilance is essential.

General Questions

1. ***Can I use my driver's license from my home country to drive in Turkey?*** **Yes.** You can generally use your valid foreign driver's license to drive in Turkey for **up to six months** from your entry date. An **International Driving Permit (IDP)** is strongly recommended, and a **notarized Turkish translation** may be required, especially if your license isn't in Latin script or you plan to stay longer. After six months—or up to one year in some cases—you must **convert your foreign license to a Turkish license** at the local Population Directorate, submitting documents like your foreign license, translation, passport or residence permit, health report, and photos. Always carry your license, IDP, and necessary documents while driving.

2. ***What is the age requirement for renting a car in Turkey?*** In Turkey, the minimum age to rent a car is **typically 21,** though this can vary depending on the rental company and vehicle category. Some agencies may require drivers to be at least 23 or 25 years old, especially for higher-end or specialty vehicles. Additionally, drivers under 25 often face a young driver surcharge, which is an extra daily fee. For example, Avis and Budget allow drivers as young as 19 to rent economy vehicles, provided they have held a valid driver's license for at least one year. However, for more premium or luxury cars, the minimum age may be 25 or older, with longer license requirements. It's important to check the specific policies of the rental company you're considering, as age and license requirements can vary.

Law of the Land Hypothetical

HYPOTHETICAL: *Ralph, a 22-year-old visitor from Canada, wants to rent a mid-size SUV in Antalya for a two-week trip. He has held his Canadian driver's license for three years. Is Ralph legally allowed to rent and drive a car in Turkey, and are there any additional fees he should expect?*

ANSWER: *In Turkey, the minimum age to rent a car is typically 21, and drivers under 25 often face a young driver surcharge, which is an extra daily fee charged by rental companies. Since Ralph is 22 and has a valid license held for over a year, he is legally allowed to rent the SUV. However, the rental company can legally charge him an additional young driver fee, which is standard practice. Ralph should confirm the amount of the surcharge and ensure his rental contract reflects this before driving.*

CHAPTER 19

NUDE BEACHES & CLOTHING-OPTIONAL RESORTS

IN THIS CHAPTER

- Overview
- Legality and Safety
- General Questions

CHAPTER 19

NUDE BEACHES & CLOTHING-OPTIONAL RESORTS

Overview

Nudism in Turkey is **not legally or culturally accepted** in the way it is in countries like Spain or Greece. Public nudity is prohibited and can lead to fines or legal trouble, as Turkey is generally conservative in its social norms. That said, in some tourist-heavy areas along the Mediterranean and Aegean coasts, a small number of foreign visitors have practiced naturism discreetly in isolated areas, though this remains unofficial and carries some risk. The only widely accepted semi-nude cultural practice is in traditional Turkish baths (hammams).

Despite these restrictions, there are certain remote beaches where nudism has been quietly practiced by visitors. **Patara Beach**, with its long and relatively empty stretch of sand, is one place where foreigners sometimes retreat to more secluded areas for nude sunbathing or swimming. **Butterfly Valley** near Fethiye, a rugged cove popular with backpackers, has also been mentioned as a spot where naturism occurs away from the main crowd. Other locations that occasionally attract naturists include **Kabak** near Fethiye, **İztuzu** near Dalyan, **Olympos** in Antalya, and some parts of **Datça**, though none of these are official or signposted as nudist friendly.

As for accommodations, Turkey does not have officially recognized naturist hotels or resorts. A few niche resorts and private villa rentals have been described online as "clothing optional" or naturist-friendly, but these are rare, discreet, and not openly advertised. Travelers interested in naturism are generally better off booking private villas with pools or seeking out very secluded beaches where they will not disturb others. Ultimately, anyone considering nudism in Turkey should approach it with caution and cultural sensitivity, as it is not part of mainstream or legal beach culture in the country.

Legality and Safety

In Turkey, nudism is not legally recognized or regulated in a formal way. Public nudity, including nude sunbathing, is generally prohibited under **laws related to public decency and morality.** Unlike in some European countries where naturism is protected or specifically zoned, Turkey has no official framework or designated areas for nudism. Practicing nudism in public spaces can therefore lead to fines, complaints from locals, or even police involvement, depending on the circumstances.

Because there are no official nudist beaches or resorts, the only places where naturism sometimes occurs are remote or hidden stretches of coastline used informally by foreign visitors. Even in those cases, it is done at personal risk since there is no legal protection. Some travelers report tolerance in very secluded spots, but this is more a matter of being discreet and avoiding public disturbance than any recognized allowance.

In most reported cases, foreigners found nude on beaches are asked to cover up immediately and may face a **monetary fine**. However, if the situation is more serious—such as repeated offenses, complaints from locals, or nudity in a family-oriented area—it can lead to being taken to a police station for questioning. In extreme circumstances, charges could result in a court appearance, which might complicate a tourist's stay or future entry into Turkey.

For this reason, both travel advisories and expat forums strongly advise against public nudism outside of the most touristy and tolerant zones. **Discretion is key**: if nudity is practiced at all, it should only be in very secluded areas or private accommodations to avoid legal issues and ensure safety.

General Questions

1. ***Is topless sunbathing allowed on Turkish beaches, especially in tourist resorts?*** **No.** Topless sunbathing is not officially permitted in Turkey, but in practice it is sometimes tolerated in heavily touristic areas along the Mediterranean and Aegean coasts, particularly around Antalya, Bodrum, and Fethiye. Even in these places, it can draw unwanted attention or complaints, as local culture is generally conservative. On family-oriented or non-tourist beaches, going topless is considered disrespectful and can lead to warnings or fines. Tourists who want to sunbathe topless should do so discreetly, ideally at private hotel pools or very secluded coves, rather than on busy public beaches.

2. ***What kinds of swimsuits are considered acceptable on Turkish beaches?*** There are no strict legal restrictions on the types of swimsuits you can wear on Turkish beaches, especially in popular tourist areas. Bikinis, one-piece swimsuits, and burkinis are all generally accepted. The main limitation is cultural: outside of beach or resort areas, wearing revealing swimwear is considered inappropriate. In more conservative regions, modest swimwear or cover-ups are recommended when leaving the beach. Essentially, as long as you stay on the beach or in resort areas, your choice of swimsuit is largely up to you, but discretion is advised when moving through towns or less touristy areas.

3. ***How is nudity handled in a traditional Turkish hammam, and what cultural norms should visitors be aware of when participating in this bathing ritual?*** In a traditional Turkish hammam, nudity is generally expected within the bathing areas, but it is treated in a non-sexual, culturally respectful way. Men and women are usually separated, and visitors are provided with a *pestemal*—a thin cotton cloth—to wrap around themselves for modesty if they feel more comfortable. Cultural norms emphasize respect for others and for the ritual itself. Full participation often involves removing swimsuits so that the attendants can perform the exfoliation and washing properly. Visitors should follow the guidance of the staff, maintain appropriate behavior, and understand that nudity in this context is about cleansing, relaxation, and tradition rather than sexual exposure.

CHAPTER 20

UNUSUAL LAWS

IN THIS CHAPTER

- Overview
- Turkey's Unusual Laws and Associated Penalties
- General Questions
- Law of the Land True Story

CHAPTER 20

UNUSUAL LAWS

Overview

Unusual laws can be fascinating glimpses into a culture's values and history. While most people are aware of common legal restrictions, it's often the strange and quirky laws that capture our attention. These regulations can range from the amusing to the absurd, reflecting the unique circumstances and traditions of a place. Whether they arise from historical events, societal norms, or simply peculiar local customs, unusual laws can provide insight into the quirks of human behavior and governance.

Turkey's Unusual Laws and Associated Penalties

- **Insulting national symbols:** Insulting the Turkish flag, national heroes, or Mustafa Kemal Atatürk is illegal. Offenders can face imprisonment ranging from 6 months to 3 years, and sometimes additional fines.
- **Mandatory id carrying:** All residents, including tourists, are required to carry identification at all times. Failure to present ID during a police check may result in fines or temporary detainment.

- **Hat law (1925):** Citizens were historically required to wear European-style hats instead of traditional fezzes as part of modernization reforms. While not actively enforced today, the law is technically still in effect.
- **Chewing gum and littering:** Spitting or disposing of chewing gum improperly in some cities is considered littering. Fines range from **₺50 to 200 ($3–$11 USD)**.
- **Animal feeding restrictions:** Feeding stray animals in certain public spaces is regulated to prevent hygiene issues. Small fines or warnings are given, usually **₺100–200 ($5–$11 USD)**.
- **No neutering your dog:** Altering an animal's reproductive capabilities is discouraged culturally. While not strictly illegal, it is frowned upon in some areas. The penalty is primarily social or administrative rather than legal.

General Questions

1. ***How strictly are unusual laws, such as those regulating public behavior or animal ownership, enforced in Turkey?*** In Turkey, the enforcement of unusual laws, such as those governing public behavior or animal ownership, varies widely across regions and depends on local authorities' priorities. For example, laws like the Animal Protection Law, which mandates microchipping, limits the number of dogs per household, and prohibits abandonment, carry fines of up to **₺10,000** (**around $1,255 USD**), but enforcement is often inconsistent due to limited municipal resources. Similarly, laws regulating public behavior, including restrictions on certain gatherings or expressions, are applied selectively, with some individuals facing penalties while others do not. This uneven enforcement reflects broader challenges in Turkey's legal system, where political, social, and economic factors can influence whether unusual laws are strictly upheld.

2. ***2. How should tourists navigate Turkey's unusual laws?***
Tourists should navigate Turkey's unusual laws by **being informed and culturally aware.** Researching local regulations before traveling, observing local customs, and following guidance from hotels, tour operators, or residents can help prevent unintentional violations. Travelers should pay attention to rules regarding public behavior, dress codes, and interactions with animals, and exercise caution when taking photos of sensitive sites or engaging in activities that could be restricted. By showing respect for local norms and laws, tourists can enjoy their visit while minimizing the risk of fines or legal issues.

Law of the Land True Story[23]

In 2014, former Miss Turkey, **Merve Buyüksarac,** shared a satirical poem on her Instagram account that parodied the Turkish national anthem and referenced a high-profile corruption scandal. Although the poem did not explicitly mention President Recep Tayyip Erdoğan, it was interpreted by authorities as insulting the president, which is a criminal offense under Article 299 of the Turkish Penal Code. This law has frequently been used to prosecute individuals, including journalists, artists, and ordinary citizens, for expressing dissenting opinions or criticism of public officials.

Buyüksarac was briefly detained and later brought to trial, where prosecutors argued that her post violated the law against insulting the president. In May 2016, she was convicted and sentenced to 14 months in prison; however, the sentence was suspended on the condition that she refrain from similar acts for the next five years. This case sparked widespread criticism from human rights organizations and free speech advocates, who viewed it as part of a broader crackdown on freedom of expression in Turkey.

23 https://www.latimes.com/world/middleeast/la-fg-turkey-beauty-queen-20160531-snap-story.html

The case highlights the delicate balance in Turkey between legal restrictions and freedom of speech. Even satirical or indirect criticism of government figures can carry serious consequences, emphasizing the need for awareness of the country's strict laws regarding public expression. It also demonstrates how legal penalties, such as suspended sentences, serve both as punishment and as a warning against future violations.

CHAPTER 21

TRAVELING SAFELY

IN THIS CHAPTER

- Ladies Traveling Solo
- Traveling as a Family
- Do's and Don'ts When Visiting Turkey

CHAPTER 21

TRAVELING SAFELY

Ladies Traveling Solo

According to the **Global Peace Index**, Turkey ranks **139 out of 163 countries**, which places it much lower than many European destinations in terms of peace and stability. That said, millions of women travel solo in Turkey every year and report positive experiences, especially in tourist-friendly areas like Istanbul, Cappadocia, Antalya, Bodrum, and Selçuk near Ephesus. Most travelers describe Turkey as **generally safe, but not without its challenges.** In major cities, popular tourist neighborhoods such as Sultanahmet and Beyoğlu in Istanbul feel comfortable, with plenty of women out and about even late in the evening. Cappadocia, coastal resorts, and historic sites are also widely considered safe and welcoming. Where issues arise is usually in less-touristed areas, late at night, or in certain neighborhoods that have a reputation for being unsafe. For example, parts of **Tarlabaşı in Istanbul** are best avoided after dark. Travelers also warn against unlicensed taxis and dolmuş minibuses when traveling alone, as scams and rare but more serious incidents have been reported.

As already discussed, **petty crime** is another concern, with pickpocketing and tourist scams common in crowded areas such as **Istanbul's Grand Bazaar or busy markets**. Overfriendly strangers offering gifts, street vendors using pressure tactics, or taxi drivers refusing to use the meter are frequent annoyances. These can usually be handled with a polite but firm refusal and by using trusted services such as ride-hailing apps.

Cultural awareness plays an important role in safety and comfort. While Turkey is not as conservative as some neighboring countries, modest clothing in rural or religious areas helps avoid unwanted attention. In cities and tourist zones, you'll see a wide range of dress styles, but covering shoulders and knees generally helps travelers blend in more easily. Women traveling solo often mention that ignoring pushy interactions, limiting eye contact with insistent strangers, and maintaining a confident demeanor make a big difference.

Beyond social concerns, travelers should be aware of **natural and political factors.** Turkey is prone to earthquakes, and wildfires occasionally disrupt travel during the summer months, although major tourist regions typically remain open and operational. Demonstrations also occur from time to time, especially in large cities, and while they are often peaceful, they can cause disruption, so it's best to avoid protest areas altogether.

Overall, Turkey is a rewarding destination for solo female travelers, with rich culture, hospitality, and incredible landscapes. While not as low risk as some other Western European countries, with planning and awareness, many women explore it independently without trouble. The key is to stay in well-reviewed accommodations, rely on trusted transportation, keep valuables secure, dress appropriately for the setting, and remain alert without being overly fearful.

Traveling as a Family

Traveling in Turkey with children is generally quite safe and enriching, though a few thoughtful precautions can help ensure a smooth and healthy family experience. Healthcare in major cities and tourist regions is robust, with public hospitals and private clinics well equipped to handle pediatric needs. It's wise to bring your child's health insurance documents and to arrange travel insurance covering children's care; also, keep a list of nearby hospitals or clinics handy in case anything arises unexpectedly. If your child requires prescription medication, bring enough for the entire trip, along with a doctor's note, as some specific brands may not be readily available in Turkey.

Regarding **vaccinations**, it's important for children to be up to date on **routine immunizations** such as MMR (measles, mumps, rubella), especially because measles remains highly contagious and has seen an uptick globally. The CDC strongly recommends children six to eleven months old traveling internationally receive one dose of MMR at least two weeks before departure, followed by the standard schedule. Additionally, **hepatitis A** vaccination is advised for all travelers, including children, to destinations with intermediate or high risk, ideally administered at least two weeks before travel. Other recommended vaccines often include **hepatitis B, flu** (if not already given during flu season), **typhoid, polio boosters,** and possibly **rabies** depending on exposure risk—your pediatrician or a travel medicine clinic like Passport Health can tailor this to your itinerary and medical history.

It's also best to err on the side of caution with tap water: while large cities like Istanbul or Ankara treat water, it's safer to **stick to bottled water** for children, especially in smaller towns or rural areas. Dining out is generally family friendly. Although formal "kid's menus" may be uncommon, many Turkish dishes—grilled meats, soups, rice, pide—are naturally suited to children's tastes and can be especially comforting.

In summer months, heat and sun are more than just mild inconveniences, especially along the Mediterranean and Aegean coasts. Be sure your children **wear sunscreen, light clothing, and hats**, and keep them well hydrated. In crowded tourist spots like bazaars, seafront promenades, or historic promenades, it's easy for little ones to become separated. ID bracelets or cards with your contact details and emergency info can provide peace of mind in bustling crowds.

When traveling with children, transport can be another area that benefits from advance planning. Car rental companies in Turkey can provide child seats if you request them ahead of time—confirm this when booking. Stroller-friendly infrastructure varies considerably: modern tram and metro systems in cities like Istanbul are accessible, but historic sites such as Cappadocia, Ephesus, or old-town quarters often feature cobblestone paths or steep terrain that can make strollers cumbersome.

It's also important to remain aware of security and health advisories affecting families. While popular tourist zones are typically calm, recent travel advice from trusted governments like the U.S., Canada, and Australia underscores that Turkey remains under **Level 2 or "exercise increased caution" advisories due to ongoing terrorism threats and civil unrest**, including large-scale protests in cities like Istanbul. Authorities recommend families avoid protests, large gatherings, and border areas near Syria or Iraq, and monitor local media closely during their stay.

Should an emergency arise, dialing 112 connects you with medical help, and English-speaking responders are more likely available near tourist centers. Your embassy can be a valuable resource; registering through programs like **STEP** (**the Smart Traveler Enrollment Program**) ensures embassy notifications and support if needed.

Do's and Don'ts While in Turkey

- **Do** greet people with a firm handshake or a friendly "Merhaba" (hello); hospitality is highly valued.
- **Don't** assume everyone speaks English; while it's common in tourist areas, learning a few Turkish phrases shows respect.
- **Do** try local dishes like kebabs, mezes, baklava, and Turkish tea or coffee — food is central to the culture.
- **Don't** drink tap water; bottled water is the safer choice, especially for visitors.
- **Do** dress modestly when visiting mosques or conservative areas — women should cover shoulders, knees, and wear a headscarf in mosques.

- **Don't** wear revealing beachwear away from the coast or poolside; it's frowned upon in public areas.
- **Do** remove your shoes before entering someone's home or a mosque — it's considered respectful.
- **Don't** sit with the soles of your feet pointing toward someone; it's seen as impolite.
- **Do** bargain politely in bazaars and markets; it's part of the experience.
- **Don't** take photos of people, especially women, without permission.
- **Do** use public transportation like trams and ferries in İstanbul — it's efficient and affordable.
- **Don't** rely solely on taxis; some drivers may overcharge, so use ride-hailing apps or agree on the fare in advance.

Turkish people are generally warm and welcoming, and visitors who show respect for local customs are often met with genuine hospitality. Accepting tea when offered is a common gesture of friendliness, and polite conversation about family, food, or travel is usually well received. Showing curiosity about the culture and traditions tends to build quick connections, while avoiding sensitive topics like politics or religion in casual encounters helps keep interactions positive.

CHAPTER 22

TOURIST TAXATION

IN THIS CHAPTER

- Overview
- Tourist Taxes in Turkey
- Law of the Land Hypothetical

CHAPTER 22

TOURIST TAXATION

Overview

Tourism plays a pivotal role in Turkey's economic framework, contributing around **12% of national GDP**, with the sector expected to reach an enormous **₺5.2 trillion (about $135.35 billion USD) in contributions in 2025**, and supporting approximately **3.3 million jobs**, which accounts for over **10% of total employment.**[24] International and domestic visitor spending are both at historic highs, illuminating tourism's vital role in economic recovery and growth. In 2024 alone, tourism revenues in Turkey climbed **8.3%**, reaching **$61.1 billion USD.**[25] The industry's impact extends beyond GDP—tourism injects much-needed foreign exchange and bolsters job markets across hospitality, transport, services, and retail.

Tourists are required to pay a **tourist tax** on most accommodation and organized travel services, implemented in January 2023. This includes hotels, motels, tourist villages, and licensed package tours. The rationale behind this tax is straightforward: to offset the extra demand placed on infrastructure and services by visitors. Tourism-heavy areas require substantial investments in maintaining historical sites, natural parks, public

24 https://wttc.org/news/turkiyes-travel-tourism-to-reach-a-record-5-point-2tn-this-year

25 https://www.reuters.com/world/middle-east/turkey-tourism-revenues-rise-83-61-bln-last-year-2025-01-31/

cleanliness, wayfinding, and safety measures. The tourist tax ensures that visitors contribute to these upkeep costs, reinforcing the sector's long-term sustainability.

Revenues collected through tourist taxation are funneled directly into **infrastructure improvement and preservation** of cultural heritage—supporting the care of iconic sites like Ephesus, Pamukkale, and Göbekli Tepe, as well as upgrading essential visitor services such as signage, emergency response systems, and environmental management.

Tourist Taxes in Turkey

In Turkey, the most significant tourist tax is the **2% national accommodation tax**, which came into effect on January 1, 2023. This tax applies to nearly all forms of overnight lodging, including hotels, holiday villages, boutique guesthouses, and campsites, as well as bundled services such as meals, spa facilities, and entertainment. It is **calculated on the base cost of the stay before VAT** and is generally added to the final bill at check-out. Accommodation providers are responsible for collecting it and transferring the amount to the Turkish Revenue Administration on a monthly basis.

Alongside this national measure, some regions such as Istanbul and Antalya have begun introducing **additional levies** that can reach 1 to 2 percent depending on the class of accommodation or location. These are not standardized across the country and can vary significantly from one municipality to another.[26] More recently, in 2025, certain upscale resort areas introduced **a flat nightly fee** of about one US dollar per guest, mainly in **four- and five-star hotels**. This is collected at check-in and earmarked for maintaining beaches, supporting eco-friendly tourism initiatives, and improving local infrastructure. Children under

26 https://theunicornforum.com/forums/topic/unveiling-turkeys-tourist-tax-a-comprehensive-guide-for-travelers

twelve are often exempt, and some hotel chains choose to cover the cost themselves.[27]

While these charges are relatively small compared to the total cost of a trip, they reflect Turkey's effort to balance the benefits of mass tourism with the environmental, cultural, and infrastructural pressures it creates. Guests should be aware that tourist taxes are typically unavoidable, though in packaged tours they may already be included in the price.

Law of the Land Hypothetical

HYPOTHETICAL: *Maria, a German tourist, books a one-week stay at a five-star resort in Antalya through an international travel agency. Her package includes accommodation, meals, and access to the resort's spa and entertainment facilities. When she checks out, she notices an additional line item on her bill labeled "accommodation tax – 2%." Maria is surprised because she believed all taxes were included in the travel agency's quoted price. The hotel insists that the tax is mandatory and must be collected from guests upon check-out. Under Turkish law, is Maria legally required to pay the 2% accommodation tax even if she booked her stay through an international travel agency and prepaid in full?*

ANSWER: **Yes.** *Maria is legally required to pay the accommodation tax. According to Turkish Law No. 7194, which introduced the accommodation tax effective January 1, 2023, all forms of paid accommodation—including hotels, holiday resorts, boutique pensions, and similar establishments—are subject to a 2% levy on the taxable amount of the stay. The responsibility to collect and remit this tax lies with the accommodation provider, not the international travel agency. Even if Maria prepaid her stay abroad, the resort is obligated by Turkish tax law to apply the accommodation tax to her bill and submit it to the Turkish Revenue Administration. Therefore, the hotel is within its*

27 https://www.evadatravel.com/en/blog/turciya-2025-5-klyuchevyh-novov-vedenij-dlya-turistov-aktualnaya-informaciya-pered-puteshestviem

legal rights to request payment at check-out. The only exception would be if Maria's travel agency contract explicitly stated that the accommodation tax was included and the resort had a prior arrangement to settle it on her behalf.

CHAPTER 23

LONG-TERM STAYS

IN THIS CHAPTER

- Overview
- Long-Term Visas
- General Questions
- Law of the Land Hypothetical
- Takeaways

CHAPTER 23
LONG-TERM STAYS

Overview

Many people choose to live long-term in Turkey because of its vibrant culture, beautiful landscapes, significantly lower cost of living, and growing healthcare system. With its Mediterranean climate, rich history, varied cuisine, and welcoming communities, Turkey can appeal to retirees, digital nomads, remote workers, and expats seeking a balanced lifestyle. The country's recent launch of a digital nomad visa further supports this trend, offering a way for qualified remote workers to legally reside in Turkey for a year or more (with the option to renew). Cities like **Istanbul, Izmir**, and smaller coastal towns such as **Dalaman, Marmaris, Antalya,** and **Fethiye** are particularly popular among long-term residents. Istanbul draws those looking for urban energy and culture, while Izmir and the Turkish Riviera offer a quieter, more relaxed setting with beautiful beaches and historical charm.

Compared to other countries, especially the United States, Turkey offers remarkably **affordable living costs.** Based on aggregated data, the average monthly cost of living in Turkey is about $898 USD per person, excluding rent—over 60% less expensive than in the U.S., where it's roughly $2,500.[28] A broader comparison shows Turkey's overall cost of living is around 52% lower than the U.S., with substantial savings on housing, food, clothing, transportation, personal care, and entertainment. While

28 https://livingcost.org/cost/turkey/united-states

these figures reflect noticeable spending power, it's important to remember that national inflation has been high in recent years, creating pressure on local salaries despite lower prices.

In addition to affordable living expenses, the **healthcare system is well-developed**, providing both public coverage and affordable private options with high standards of care. Since 2003, the country offers universal health insurance known as **"Genel Sağlık Sigortası,"** financed through employer contributions and taxes, with the system covering a broad range of services including emergency care, childbirth, preventive services, and certain medications. Public services are widely available, and private healthcare—often faster and more specialized—is also affordable compared to many Western countries.

Long-term living offers **diverse housing opportunities**, from modern high-rises in Istanbul to quaint apartments along the Aegean Coast. Rent for a modest one-bedroom city-center apartment in cities like Istanbul or Izmir generally ranges from **$300 USD to $500 USD per month,** with utilities roughly **$50–$100 monthly**—well below what many expats pay in major U.S. cities.[29] **Public transport** is **efficient and budget friendly**. A single ride often costs less than a dollar, while monthly passes are sometimes as low as $20 USD, making everyday travel both convenient and affordable.

And lastly, language is another important consideration. **English is commonly spoken** in tourist areas and among younger people in cities like Istanbul and Izmir, which helps newcomers navigate daily life. At the same time, learning some Turkish can greatly enrich the long-term experience, making it easier to build relationships with locals, access services outside of major cities, and feel more integrated into the culture. Many expats find that the warmth and hospitality of Turkish people make the process of practicing and learning the language enjoyable, adding to the sense of community and belonging that makes Turkey an appealing place to settle for the long term.

29 https://sirelo.com/moving-abroad/moving-to-turkey

Long-Term Visas

Turkey has become an increasingly attractive destination for long-term living, offering a blend of cultural richness, natural beauty, affordability, and strategic location between Europe and Asia. To accommodate the diverse needs of foreigners wishing to stay beyond short visits, Turkey provides a range of visa and residence options. Whether you are a retiree seeking a peaceful lifestyle, a digital nomad working remotely, an investor looking for opportunities, or a family wishing to settle, Turkey's long-term visas and permits make it possible to enjoy life in the country legally and securely.

Short-term residence permit (e-ikamet):

The Short-Term Residence Permit is one of the most flexible options and can be granted for **up to two years, with the possibility of indefinite renewal.** It is often chosen by retirees, property owners, or individuals wishing to stay in Turkey without formal employment. Applicants must provide proof of sufficient financial means, a registered address in Turkey, and valid health insurance.

Digital nomad visa:

Introduced recently, the Digital Nomad Visa is designed for remote workers and freelancers. It allows individuals from eligible countries, aged **21 to 55**, to live and work in Turkey **for one year, with the option to renew**. Applicants must hold a university degree, show proof of remote employment or self-employment with foreign clients, and demonstrate a **minimum monthly income of around $3,000 USD.** Successful applicants first obtain a Digital Nomad Identification Certificate before completing the visa process through a Turkish consulate.

Property-based residence permit:

Foreigners who purchase real estate in Turkey may qualify for a residence permit. This permit is **valid for two years and renewable as long as the property is retained.** Regulations require a minimum residential real estate investment of approximately **$175,000 USD** to qualify. This option is popular among those wishing to combine investment with lifestyle, particularly in coastal cities and resort areas.

Work permit:

Foreign nationals with a job offer in Turkey can apply for a Work Permit, which also functions as a residence permit. These permits are typically valid for **one to two years and can be extended.** Turkey also offers the **Turquoise Card program**, similar to an EU Blue Card, which grants long-term rights to highly skilled professionals, investors, or entrepreneurs. Over time, work permit holders may transition toward permanent residence or even citizenship.

Family residence permit:

Spouses and dependent children of Turkish citizens or legal residents can apply for a Family Residence Permit. Valid for **up to three years**, this permit allows family members to live together in Turkey and access education and healthcare services. It is **renewable** as long as the sponsoring family member maintains their legal status.

Long-term residence permit:

After residing legally in Turkey for at least eight continuous years, foreigners may apply for a Long-Term Residence Permit. This permit grants **indefinite residency**, offering nearly all the rights of Turkish citizens, with the exception of voting and military service obligations. It is ideal for those who wish to permanently settle in Turkey.

Citizenship by investment (golden visa equivalent):

Turkey's Citizenship by Investment program allows eligible foreigners to fast-track their way to citizenship. The most popular option requires investing at least **$400,000 USD in real estate** and holding it for three years. Alternatives include **depositing $500,000 USD** in a Turkish bank, **purchasing government bonds**, or **investing in job-creating**

enterprises. Successful applicants and their families can acquire Turkish passports within a relatively short timeframe.

To acquire a long-term visa or residence permit in Turkey, applicants generally need a valid passport with sufficient remaining validity and must demonstrate adequate financial means to support themselves and any dependents without relying on public funds. Proof of comprehensive health insurance covering the entire stay is required, along with a registered residential address in Turkey, typically verified through a rental agreement or property ownership documents. Applicants must provide documentation supporting the purpose of their stay, such as a job contract for work permits, proof of remote employment for digital nomads, enrollment in an educational institution for students, or property ownership for investment-based permits. A clean criminal record is usually required, and applicants must pay administrative fees associated with their application. Certain visas may have age or eligibility limits, and for permits that lead to long-term residence or citizenship, maintaining continuous legal stay in Turkey is essential. Each visa type also carries additional specific criteria, but these general requirements form the foundation for obtaining long-term residency in the country.

General Questions

1. ***If I plan to live in Turkey long-term and work, do I need to obtain a work permit before entering the country?*** **Yes.** Generally you should apply for a work permit **before** arriving in Turkey. Most work permits are processed by the Turkish authorities in advance, and you typically cannot start working legally without one. Some visa types allow you to enter Turkey first and apply from within the country, but starting employment without the proper permit is not allowed and could result in fines, deportation, or difficulties obtaining future residency. It's important to coordinate with your prospective employer and ensure all necessary documentation is submitted according to Turkish labor and immigration regulations before your arrival.

2. ***I am American. Can I retire to Turkey?* Yes.** As an American, you can retire to Turkey. To do so legally, you would typically apply for a long-term residence permit or a specific retirement visa. You need to show proof of sufficient income or savings to support yourself without working in Turkey, and you may also need to provide health insurance coverage. Once approved, this permit allows you to live in Turkey long-term and enjoy the benefits of residing in the country as a retiree.

Law of the Land Hypothetical

HYPOTHETICAL: *James, a freelance graphic designer from Canada, wants to live in Istanbul while continuing to work remotely for clients abroad. He is unsure which visa or permit will allow him to stay in Turkey legally while earning income from outside the country.*

ANSWER: *James can apply for a long-term residence permit in Turkey, and he may also be eligible for a work authorization that allows him to work as a remote freelancer for foreign clients. He must provide proof of sufficient income or savings to support himself without relying on local employment, evidence of accommodation in Turkey, valid health insurance, and a valid passport. The application is submitted through the local Directorate General of Migration Management. Once approved, this permit enables him to reside legally in Turkey, conduct remote work for international clients, and renew his residency annually, providing a stable framework for long-term living while maintaining his freelance business.*

Takeaways

Turkey offers a combination of vibrant culture, Mediterranean climate, historical charm, and lower living costs, making it appealing to retirees, digital nomads, remote workers, and expats.

Long-term residents can find affordable apartments, from city-center flats in Istanbul to coastal properties, while public transportation is convenient and budget-friendly.

Turkey has a well-developed healthcare system, including universal coverage and affordable private options, ensuring access to quality medical care for residents.

Turkey provides a range of permits and visas for different purposes—short-term, work, digital nomad, property-based, family, long-term residency, and citizenship by investment—allowing foreigners to stay legally and securely.

To obtain long-term residency, applicants generally need a valid passport, proof of financial means, comprehensive health insurance, a registered address, supporting documents based on their visa type, a clean criminal record, and compliance with age or eligibility criteria for specific permits.

CHAPTER 24

CIVIL LITIGATION

IN THIS CHAPTER

- Overview
- Personal Injury Claims and Compensation Law
- How to File a Civil Claim
- Service of Documents
- Statute of Limitations
- Getting Married in Turkey
- Law of the Land Hypothetical

CHAPTER 24

CIVIL LITIGATION

Overview

Civil litigation provides a mechanism for resolving disputes, ensuring that travelers have a way to seek justice if legal issues arise while visiting another country. It helps them understand their rights and obligations under local laws, which may differ from those in their home country. The civil litigation system offers a formal process for addressing conflicts, such as contract disputes or personal injury claims, and can deter unfair practices by encouraging businesses to comply with legal standards. It also allows individuals to seek financial recourse for damages or losses and helps protect them from potential exploitation by local entities. Overall, understanding civil litigation enhances a visitor's experience and safety while traveling.

Personal Injury Claims and Compensation Law[30]

Personal injury claims and compensation law in Turkey are designed to ensure that individuals who suffer harm due to the fault or negligence of another party receive appropriate compensation. A personal injury claim in Turkey can arise when an individual is injured as a result of **traffic accidents, workplace accidents, medical malpractice, unsafe**

30 https://www.firatfesihkaya.av.tr/how-to-file-a-personal-injury-compensation-claim-in-turkey/

conditions on someone else's property, or defective products. The injured party must demonstrate that the harm was caused by another's negligence or wrongful act.

After an injury, it is essential to **seek medical attention immediately**, even for minor injuries, as medical records will be crucial for any claim. The **incident should be reported** to the appropriate authorities, such as the police or, in the case of workplace injuries, the employer. It is also important to **document the incident thoroughly**, including photographs of the scene and injuries, witness statements, and any communications with insurance companies. Consulting a lawyer who specializes in personal injury law can provide guidance throughout the process and help ensure that fair compensation is sought.

Compensation for personal injuries in Turkey is calculated based on several factors, including medical costs, lost income, economic losses, and non-pecuniary damages such as pain, suffering, emotional distress, and loss of quality of life. The severity of the injury, permanence of the harm, age of the victim, and psychological impact are considered when determining compensation. While medical and economic damages have clearer benchmarks, non-pecuniary damages are determined on a case-by-case basis through Turkish case law.

Insurance plays a significant role in personal injury claims in Turkey. Many individuals and businesses carry insurance that covers the costs of such claims. For instance, **Compulsory Traffic Insurance (Zorunlu Trafik Sigortası)** covers third-party injuries in traffic accidents up to statutory limits, allowing victims to file claims directly with the at-fault party's insurer before resorting to litigation. If the responsible party lacks insurance or coverage is insufficient, legal avenues still exist to pursue compensation.

Legal fees for personal injury claims in Turkey vary depending on the case's complexity and the lawyer's fee structure. It is common for lawyers to operate on a "no win, no fee" basis, charging a percentage of the awarded compensation, typically **between 10% and 25%.** Additional costs may include court fees and expert evaluations, such as medical reports. Navigating personal injury claims requires careful documentation, understanding of Turkish law, and professional legal support to ensure a fair outcome for the injured party.

How to File a Civil Claim

Filing a civil claim in Turkey is governed by the **Turkish Civil Procedure Code** (**Law No. 6100**) and requires meeting specific procedural conditions. To start a claim, the petitioner must submit a **written petition** to the competent court, which must include the full names and addresses of all parties involved, a clear summary of the facts leading to the dispute, the legal grounds for the claim, the specific remedy or relief sought, and a list of supporting evidence.

If the claimant is represented by a lawyer, a **notarized power of attorney** must also be submitted. Foreign documents must be certified, translated into Turkish, and may require notarization or apostille depending on their origin.

Civil claims in Turkey can involve a variety of disputes. Ordinary proceedings are used for complex cases or claims exceeding a certain monetary threshold, while simplified procedures apply to disputes below specified amounts or certain types of claims such as labor disputes. Some matters are handled by specialized courts, including Family Courts, Consumer Courts, and Labor Courts.

Essential documents for filing a civil claim include the written petition (dava dilekçesi), supporting evidence such as contracts, invoices, correspondence, notarized power of attorney if represented by a lawyer, certified translations of foreign documents, and proof of payment of any applicable court fees. The court in which the claim should be filed is determined by factors such as the defendant's domicile or habitual residence, the location where the contractual obligation was to be performed, or the place where the event giving rise to the dispute occurred. In cases involving multiple defendants, the lawsuit may be filed in the court of the domicile of any of the defendants.

Additional considerations include filing the claim within **statutory limitation periods** (discussed below), as missing these deadlines can result in dismissal, and following the principle of territorial proximity, which ensures the case is filed in court near the defendant's residence or where the legal event occurred. Foreigners filing a claim in Turkey must ensure all documents are properly translated and notarized, making it highly advisable to consult a Turkish lawyer to navigate procedural requirements effectively. Understanding these requirements is essential to successfully initiating a civil claim in Turkey and ensuring that legal proceedings proceed smoothly.

Service of Documents[31]

The service of documents in Turkey is governed by the **Turkish Code of Civil Procedure (Law No. 6100)** and, in international cases, by the **Hague Service Convention of 1965**, which Turkey has ratified but with a reservation against postal service under Article 10. Domestically, service is handled by **court officers or authorized process servers** under court supervision to ensure that parties receive formal notice in compliance with procedural law. In cross-border cases, requests must be sent to the **Turkish Ministry of Justice** as the designated Central Authority, accompanied by translated copies of the documents, which are then served through local courts in accordance with Turkish procedures.

The process begins with the preparation of the legal documents to be served, which must be translated into Turkish if originating abroad. For domestic cases, the court issues the documents and assigns an official to deliver them personally to the recipient or, if unavailable, to another eligible individual at their address as allowed by law. In international cases, once the Ministry of Justice receives the request, it instructs the competent local court to carry out service and returns confirmation to the requesting authority.

Proof of service is recorded through an **official certificate** prepared by the serving officer or court clerk, detailing the method, date, and

31 https://stellarkonsulting.com/international-process-service/turkey

recipient of delivery; in Hague Convention cases, a formal certificate of service is provided to the requesting state. This ensures that service complies with Turkish procedural requirements and is recognized as valid in domestic and international proceedings.

Statute of Limitations

In Turkey, the statute of limitations for civil claims—referred to as "**extinctive prescription**"—is governed by the **Turkish Code of Obligations (Law No. 6098)**. The general limitation period for most claims is **ten years**, starting from the moment the obligation becomes due. If no specific limitation is prescribed by law, this ten-year period applies.

Certain types of claims, however, are subject to a **shorter limitation period of five years.** These include **periodic obligations** such as rent, salary, and interest; debts arising from agency, commission, or brokerage agreements (excluding commercial brokerage); claims related to partnership agreements and management or auditor relationships; hotel accommodation fees; catering costs at restaurants; small-scale retail sales; minor artistry work; and works contracts—unless the claim concerns grossly negligent or improper performance.

Tort claims, including compensation for non-contractual liability, are generally subject to a **two-year limitation period** that begins from the date the injured party becomes aware of the damage, the tortious act, and the identity of the responsible party—but in any event, the claim must be brought within ten years from the date the wrongful act itself occurred.

Beyond this, specific laws may set **different limitation periods for particular types of disputes.** For instance, claims arising from **unjust enrichment** are treated similarly to tort claims, with a **two-year limitation** starting from when the claimant becomes aware of the enrichment and the liable party, capped at ten years from the enrichment event. In commercial law, the Turkish Commercial Code dictates, for example, that **unfair competition claims** must be brought within **one year** of learning of the violation—but no later than three years after the act occurred.

Transport-related claims vary: **bodily injury** or death of a passenger must be claimed within **ten years**, while **cargo or delivery-related damages** generally have **a one-year period** (extended to three years if the carrier acted intentionally or recklessly). **Insurance claims** fall under a **ten-year period** from the insured event.

Employment-related claims such as unpaid wages, bonuses, and similar entitlements have a **five-year limitation** under the Labor Law, and wrongful dismissal claims must adhere to mediation and lawsuit timeframes—typically one month for mediation, followed by two weeks to file suit if mediation fails. Under the Consumer Protection Law, liability for **consumer goods defects** expires **two years after delivery** (unless longer by law or contract), with five-year limits for residential or vacation property defects; second-hand sales cannot limit seller liability to less than one year—or three years for property—unless the defect was fraudulently concealed.

These limitation periods are considered substantive legal matters. Courts do not raise them on their own motion; a defendant must explicitly plead expiry of the limitation as a defense, or risk forfeiting the defense entirely.

Moreover, the statute of limitations can be **interrupted** by certain actions: filing a lawsuit, initiating enforcement or bankruptcy proceedings, arbitration, or even partial payment or acknowledging the debt—all of which reset the limitation clock. In construction or commercial contexts, such interruptions can restart the period, often extending it to the full ten-year term again.

In summary, Turkey's approach to civil limitation periods is structured yet nuanced. The general rule grants ten years unless the law specifies otherwise—usually five years for routine economic or contract-related claims, and two years (with a ten-year cap) for tort and similar claims. These limitations vary depending on subject matter—ranging from consumer goods to employment, transport, and insurance—and can be paused or reset through specific legal or procedural actions.

Getting Married in Turkey

Turkey has increasingly become known as an international wedding destination, attracting couples from Europe, the Middle East, Asia, and beyond due to its unique blend of cultural heritage, scenic landscapes, and relatively straightforward legal process for foreigners. Iconic locations such as Istanbul's Bosphorus waterfront, Cappadocia's fairy chimneys, Antalya's Mediterranean beaches, and Bodrum's luxury resorts make it a sought-after spot for destination weddings. The country offers a combination of modern facilities, historical charm, and competitive costs compared to many Western countries, which has boosted its popularity for both intimate civil ceremonies and elaborate celebrations.

To marry legally in Turkey, **civil marriage is the only recognized form**—any religious ceremony must follow a civil wedding to have legal effect. Both partners must be **at least 18**, though 17-year-olds may marry with parental consent, and 16-year-olds only under exceptional circumstances and with court approval. The couple must have full legal capacity, meaning neither is currently married nor closely related. Foreign nationals and Turkish citizens alike can marry, and there is no strict residency requirement—visitors can marry—but the foreign party must be in legal stay (valid visa or residence permit).

Key documents include **valid passports** (translated to Turkish and notarized), a **Certificate of No Impediment or Certificate of Celibacy** proving freedom to marry (and, if needed, a birth certificate with parental names), all of which must be apostilled or consularly legalized—and then translated by a sworn translator and notarized in Turkey. A **health report with a blood test** from a state health institution is mandatory. Typically, 4–6 recent passport-size photos are required. If a partner has been previously married, divorce decrees or death certificates must be submitted, similarly legalized and translated.

The process begins with both partners appearing in person at the local Marriage Office—'Evlendirme Dairesi'—where one resides and submitting the marriage application (petition), along with all documentation. The office verifies the paperwork and issues the marriage license.

The civil ceremony must include two adult witnesses and, if needed, a certified Turkish-language interpreter. Once conducted by a marriage officer ('Nikah Memuru'), the couple receives the official marriage certificate, known as the *Evlenme Cüzdanı*. Religious ceremonies are optional and have no legal force unless preceded by the civil ceremony.

Timing varies: once documents are ready and the office schedules them, marriage can occur within a few days to a week. In busy seasons or municipalities, it may take longer. In some regions, a mandated waiting period (e.g. one day) may apply before the ceremony.

Fees typically include **administrative charges, translation, notarization, and medical tests.** As a rough estimate, marriage application fees may be around $50–$100 USD, notary and translation cost $50–$150 USD, health checks $20–$50 USD, and the ceremony or venue can vary widely—from under $500 USD for a basic office wedding to thousands for upscale settings. Locals have reported nominal government fees—for example, in Istanbul it could be ₺600 (around $160 USD) for two foreign nationals marrying.

There have been recent discussions that foreign nationals might now need a residence permit to marry. However, this doesn't have confirmed official backing, and many local registrars and embassies still indicate a valid passport and visa are sufficient. Enforcement appears inconsistent by city, so it's wise to check with your local Nikah Dairesi (local marriage office) or consulate.

Law of the Land Hypothetical

HYPOTHETICAL: *Emma, a British tourist, slips and falls on a wet floor in the lobby of a luxury hotel in Antalya. There was no warning sign posted, and she suffers a fractured ankle, forcing her to cancel the rest of her holiday and incur significant medical expenses. The hotel manager apologizes but refuses to cover her costs, claiming that since she is a foreign visitor she has no real recourse. Can Emma file a personal injury claim against the hotel in Turkey even though she's not a resident?*

ANSWER: **Yes.** *Emma can file a personal injury claim in Turkey despite being a non-resident because Turkish law grants the right to seek compensation for harm caused by another's negligence to anyone within its jurisdiction, including tourists. Her claim would fall under tort liability, requiring proof that the hotel breached its duty of care by failing to provide a safe environment and that this directly caused her injury. Evidence such as medical reports from the Turkish hospital, photographs of the accident scene, witness statements from other guests, and hotel records will strengthen her case.*

The claim would typically be filed in the civil court located where the injury occurred—in Antalya. She can hire a Turkish attorney to represent her without needing to remain in Turkey, granting them authority via a notarized and apostilled power of attorney. The lawyer can negotiate with the hotel's insurer first, as many hotels carry liability coverage, and if no settlement is reached, proceed with litigation. Compensation could include medical expenses, lost enjoyment of her trip, pain and suffering, and potentially lost income if she missed work. The statute of limitations for such a claim is generally two years from the date of injury, so she must act promptly.

CHAPTER 25

OTHER THINGS TO KNOW

IN THIS CHAPTER

- Tourists and Street Hustling
- Safety Concerns and Practical Tips
- In the Event of Death
- Experiencing Financial Hardship

CHAPTER 25

OTHER THINGS TO KNOW

Tourists and Street Hustling

Street hustling is **fairly common** in major Turkish tourist destinations like Istanbul, Antalya, Cappadocia, and Konya, where crowds and unfamiliar surroundings create ideal conditions for opportunistic scammers. Hustlers frequently engage in behaviors such as overly friendly approaches, excessive selling pressure, and staged distractions. They may drop brushes near you to prompt a "courtesy" shoeshine that ends with an inflated bill, a notorious tactic in cities like Istanbul and Cappadocia. Tourists may also be tempted with fake ancient coins or artifacts near historic sites or lured into buying overpriced carpets from street vendors with misleading authenticity claims. Aggressive tactics aren't limited to goods—solicitors may invite you for a "local drink" or free tea, only to present an astronomical bill at the end.

Street hustlers also include fake guides and photographers who offer unsolicited help or take your picture, then demand payment or trick you into damaging (or pretending to damage) their equipment. Other tactics include the "spilling something on you" distraction used to divert your attention while pickpockets strike, as well as scams targeting ATM users or involving currency exchange tricks, like charging in euros instead of lira or using sleight of hand with cash.

Popular tourist hubs, particularly **Istanbul's Grand Bazaar, Sultanahmet, Spice Bazaar, Taksim Square, and Antalya's old town,** are hotspots for street hustling due to their high visitor traffic and crowded spaces that allow scammers to operate under cover.

Local authorities and tourism bodies have taken steps to tackle these issues. After several high-profile incidents, Turkish officials prosecuted operators of deceptive "clip joint" tours and tightened regulations against tour touts who pressure visitors into buying goods like carpets. There are established hotlines such as the **Tourist Police**, and **general police** are available to report scams. Travel guides and tourism agencies strongly advise visitors to **remain vigilant, verify prices upfront, avoid unsolicited help, and report suspicious activity promptly**.

Safety Concerns and Practical Tips

Interacting with street hustlers in Turkey can create several safety concerns for tourists. Such encounters may result in theft, scams, or aggressive confrontations, as hustlers often use distraction techniques to divert attention while accomplices pickpocket or manipulate tourists. In some instances, persistent solicitation or refusal to comply with demands for payment can escalate into verbal or even physical harassment. Tourists unfamiliar with local tactics, like the "spilling something on you" trick or unsolicited photo opportunities, are particularly vulnerable.

To protect themselves, visitors should remain alert in crowded tourist areas, keeping personal belongings secure and avoiding the display of valuables. Politely but firmly declining offers, walking away from overly insistent vendors, and not engaging in impromptu games or purchases from strangers can significantly reduce risk. Using common-sense precautions like carrying only necessary cash, maintaining situational awareness, and traveling with companions also helps minimize potential problems.

Understanding local customs and behaviors can further assist tourists in safely navigating street interactions. For example, aggressive solicitation is generally not considered socially acceptable, and most local vendors respect a firm refusal. Learning basic Turkish phrases such as **"Hayır, teşekkür ederim"** (**"No, thank you"**) can be useful for asserting boundaries politely. Observing how locals interact with street vendors and following their lead in public spaces can also provide subtle guidance.

If harassment, theft, or scams occur, tourists can report incidents to the Tourist Police or the general police by dialing **155**. Embassies and consulates are available for guidance and support, especially in cases involving legal disputes or lost documents. Many municipalities also provide online resources or local tourist information centers where visitors can seek advice on avoiding scams and recording complaints, ensuring they have recourse if needed.

In the Event of Death

If someone traveling with you dies while in Turkey, it is crucial to act promptly and follow both local and consular procedures. The first step is to **notify local emergency services by calling 112**. Once the authorities arrive, the police and a medical professional—usually a forensic doctor—will examine the deceased and issue an official death certificate.

Following this, you should immediately **contact your country's embassy or consulate** in Turkey. Consular staff can assist with identifying the deceased, notifying next of kin, explaining local procedures, and coordinating with Turkish authorities and funeral service providers. The embassy or consulate cannot pay for funeral or transport costs, but they can provide guidance on obtaining official documents, translation services, and liaising with local funeral homes. If the family wishes to repatriate the deceased's remains, a licensed Turkish funeral director must prepare the body for transport and secure the necessary permits, including an international death certificate and a mortuary passport. Repatriation typically requires embalming and sealing the body in a hermetically closed casket to comply with both Turkish and international transport regulations.

Families should be aware that the cost of repatriation from Turkey can vary widely, often ranging from $3,000 USD to $6,000 USD depending on services, location, and airline requirements. Travel insurance policies may cover some or all of these expenses, so verifying coverage is recommended. Alternatively, local burial or cremation in Turkey is legally permitted and may involve fewer logistical challenges. It is important to **register the death both with local authorities in Turkey and with the deceased's home country**, a process the consulate can help facilitate to ensure all legal and administrative requirements are met.

Experiencing Financial Hardship

Tourists in Turkey may face financial hardship for several reasons, including theft of wallets or cards, unexpected medical or travel expenses, loss of cash, or frozen bank accounts due to suspected fraud. Language barriers or limited access to online banking can make it difficult to resolve financial problems quickly. If a traveler runs out of money, the first step should be to contact their bank to explore emergency cash transfers or temporary card solutions, which can often be facilitated through services like Western Union or MoneyGram, available in most major Turkish cities and tourist areas. Travelers should also contact their country's embassy or consulate, which cannot provide direct financial assistance but can help coordinate money transfers from family or friends and offer guidance on local support resources.

Turkey has support systems for travelers facing hardship. Tourist assistance services and centers in major cities such as Istanbul, Antalya, and Cappadocia can provide multilingual help for victims of theft, scams, or other emergencies. Some charitable organizations, NGOs, or local religious institutions may also offer short-term aid, including food, temporary shelter, or guidance on emergency services.

Understanding local costs and currency is crucial for managing expenses. The Turkish lira (₺) is the national currency, and prices vary by region and season. A basic meal typically costs around ₺150–250 ($8–$14 USD), public transportation fares range from ₺15–30 ($0.80–$1.60 USD) per ride, and mid-range hotels generally cost ₺1,500–3,000 ($80–$160 USD) per night. Having both a physical and digital backup payment method is highly recommended, as is familiarizing oneself with approximate costs for accommodation, food, transport, and attractions to avoid unexpected overspending.

To manage expenses effectively, tourists should budget daily spending, track costs using apps, carry a mix of cash and cards without holding large amounts, take advantage of free or low-cost attractions such as museums with free entry days or public parks, and minimize ATM fees by limiting frequent withdrawals. Awareness of local pricing and preparation for unexpected costs can significantly reduce financial stress while traveling in Turkey.

CHAPTER 26

QUICK REFERENCE GUIDE

IN THIS CHAPTER

- Quick Chapter References to Important Topics

CHAPTER 26

QUICK REFERENCE GUIDE

Crime in Turkey

Are there particular areas I should avoid as a tourist?

Yes. While Turkey is generally safe for tourists, especially in popular spots like Istanbul, Antalya, Bodrum, and Cappadocia, some areas are best avoided. Regions near the Syrian and Iraqi borders, such as Şırnak and Hakkari, pose security risks due to terrorism and conflict. In Istanbul, neighborhoods like Dolapdere, Tarlabaşı, Esenyurt, Kasımpaşa, Kuştepe, Gülsuyu, Laleli-Aksaray, and Gaziosmanpaşa have higher crime rates, while parts of İstiklal Avenue are known for scams and hustlers. Environmental risks like wildfires and earthquakes also exist. Sticking to well-lit, busy areas, securing valuables, avoiding unlicensed transport, and monitoring local advisories can help ensure a safe and enjoyable visit. *For more details, see Chapter 3.*

Drug Offenses

Is the possession of marijuana legal?

No. Marijuana possession is strictly **illegal** in Turkey, with penalties of two to five years in prison even for small amounts, though first-time offenders may be placed on probation or required to undergo treatment. Selling, supplying, or trafficking cannabis carries much harsher sentences, often exceeding ten years. **Medical marijuana** is

limited to specific prescription drugs like Sativex, with recreational use entirely banned. Tourists are subject to the same laws and face serious consequences if caught.

Is the possession of cocaine legal?

No. The possession of cocaine is strictly **illegal** in Turkey. It is classified as a serious narcotic, and anyone caught with it faces severe criminal penalties, including lengthy prison sentences. The laws apply equally to tourists and locals, and there is no allowance for personal or recreational use. *For more details, see Chapter 4.*

Alcohol-Related Offenses

What is the legal drinking age?

The legal drinking age in Turkey is **18**. Alcohol can be purchased and consumed by anyone 18 or older, but there are restrictions on where and when it can be sold, such as bans on sales after 10 p.m. and limitations near schools and mosques.

What is the legal blood alcohol limit?

In Turkey, the legal blood alcohol concentration limit is **0.50 g/L** (**0.05%**) for **private car drivers**. For **professional or commercial drivers and motorcycle drivers**, the limit is **0.00 g/L** (**0.00%**). Exceeding these limits can result in fines, license suspension, and other penalties. *For more details, see Chapter 5.*

Firearm & Ammunition Offenses

Can I possess a gun?

Yes. In Turkey, you can possess a gun, but there are **strict regulations**. You must have a valid firearm license, which is issued only under certain conditions, such as proving a legitimate need for self-defense, hunting, or sport shooting, passing a background check, and completing required safety training. Certain people, like those with criminal records or certain mental health issues, are prohibited from owning firearms.

Can I possess ammunition?

Yes. In Turkey you can possess ammunition, but **only if you have a valid firearm license.** Ammunition possession is strictly tied to the type and number of firearms you are legally allowed to own. Carrying or storing ammunition without the appropriate license is illegal and can lead to criminal penalties. *For more details, see Chapter 6.*

Prostitution

Is prostitution legal?

Yes. In Turkey, prostitution is **legal but highly regulated**. It is only permitted in licensed brothels, and sex workers must be registered with health authorities and undergo regular medical checks. Street prostitution and unlicensed sexual services are illegal and can lead to fines, arrest, or other penalties. *For more details, see Chapter 7.*

LGBTQ

Is homosexuality legal?

Yes. Homosexuality is **legal** in Turkey. Consensual same-sex sexual activity between adults is not criminalized. However, there are **no legal protections against discrimination** based on sexual orientation, and social acceptance can vary widely depending on the region.

Are same sex public displays of affection legal?

There is no specific law in Turkey that criminalizes same-sex public displays of affection (PDA), so technically they are **not illegal.** However, in practice, such behavior can attract **harassment, fines, or police attention**, especially in more conservative areas. Public acceptance varies greatly between cities; larger cities like Istanbul or Ankara tend to be more tolerant than rural areas. *For more details, see Chapter 8.*

Arrested in Turkey

Would I be entitled to bail if I'm arrested?

In Turkey, whether you are entitled to bail **depends on the nature of the alleged offense** and the circumstances of your arrest. For many minor offenses, a judge can grant **release pending trial**, sometimes with conditions such as reporting to the police or surrendering your passport. However, for serious crimes—especially violent crimes, drug trafficking, or offenses deemed a threat to public order—pre-trial detention is common, and bail may be **denied.**

Will a lawyer be provided to me if I cannot afford one?

Yes. In Turkey, if you are arrested and cannot afford a lawyer, the court will **appoint a public defender** to represent you. This applies to both Turkish citizens and foreigners. You have the right to consult with your lawyer before and during questioning, and the lawyer can attend court hearings on your behalf. *For more details, see Chapter 10.*

Helping a Friend or Relative Imprisoned in Turkey

Can I send money to a friend or family member imprisoned in Turkey?

Yes. You can send money to a friend or family member imprisoned in Turkey, but it must be done through official channels. Funds are typically deposited into the inmate's prison account or used to purchase items from the prison shop, and cash sent by mail is not allowed. International bank transfers may be possible, but it's important to confirm with the specific prison and ensure the transfer complies with Turkish laws, as transactions to prisoners can be legally scrutinized.

Can I remain in Turkey upon release from prison or jail after my sentence is complete?

Yes. You can remain in Turkey after completing your prison sentence, but it depends on your **residency or visa status**. If you are a foreign national, your permission to stay is tied to your visa, residence permit, or other immigration status. Completing a sentence does **not automatically grant you the right to stay**, and in some cases, foreign prisoners may be **subject to deportation** after release. It's important to check with Turkish immigration authorities or a lawyer to understand your options for extending your stay legally. *For more details, see Chapter 12.*

Crime Victim Assistance

Can a victim of a crime be legally compensated?

Yes. In Turkey, a victim of a crime can seek legal compensation. This can be done through a **criminal case**, where the court may order the offender to pay restitution, or through a **civil lawsuit** for damages, including medical expenses, lost income, or emotional distress. Victims can also apply for state-supported compensation in certain cases, such as violent crimes, if the offender cannot pay. The process usually requires filing a claim with the court and providing evidence of the harm suffered. *For more details, see Chapter 14.*

U.S. Consulate Assistance

Are there any limitations to the consulate assistance I can receive while in Turkey?

Yes. While the U.S. Embassy and Consulates in Turkey provide essential assistance to U.S. citizens, there are specific limitations to the support they can offer. They can help with emergencies such as lost passports, arrests, medical issues, or if you're a victim of crime. However, they cannot intervene in Turkish legal matters, including criminal or civil cases, or assist with Turkish immigration or visa issues . Additionally, consular services do not extend to pets or personal property matters. *For more details, see Chapter 14.*

Police

Is there an official police force?

Yes. Turkey has an official police force known as the **Turkish National Police** (**Emniyet Genel Müdürlüğü**), responsible for maintaining public order, enforcing laws, investigating crimes, and ensuring the safety of citizens and residents. In addition to the national police, there is the **Gendarmerie** (**Jandarma**), which handles law enforcement in rural areas and regions outside city limits. Both forces operate under the Ministry of Interior and have the authority to arrest, investigate, and detain individuals suspected of committing crimes. *For more details, see Chapter 15.*

How to Get Legal Help in Turkey

Is there a resource in Turkey to find legal representation?

In Turkey, you can find legal representation through local **Bar Associations**, which maintain lawyer directories and offer free legal aid for those who qualify financially. Major cities like Istanbul, Ankara, and Izmir have searchable online directories. **Online legal platforms** like Advocate Abroad, Pi Legal Consultancy, and ER Law Firm connect clients with English-speaking lawyers. Specialized organizations, such as **UNHCR Türkiye**, **Mor Çatı Foundation**, and **SPoD**, provide legal support to refugees, women, and LGBTI+ individuals. The **Ministry of Justice** and the **Ombudsman Institution** also provide guidance on legal aid and lawyer access. When choosing a lawyer, consider specialization, language, reputation, and consultation options.

Does the US embassy provide a list of local attorneys that speak English?

Yes. The U.S. Embassy in Turkey provides a list of local attorneys who speak English. This list includes lawyers who have expressed interest in assisting U.S. citizens and have been vetted by the embassy. While the embassy does not endorse any specific attorney, the list serves as a helpful resource for finding legal representation in Turkey. You can access the list of English-speaking attorneys on the U.S. Embassy's official website at **https://tr.usembassy.gov/legal-assistance.** *For more details, see Chapter 16.*

Foreign Embassies in Turkey

Are there foreign embassies in Turkey?

Yes. Turkey hosts foreign embassies from nearly every country, with most located in Ankara, the capital and main diplomatic hub. Major cities like Istanbul also have consulates and honorary consulates representing various countries. These embassies provide services such as visa and passport processing, assistance to citizens abroad, legal and emergency support, and facilitating trade, cultural, and diplomatic relations. Countries like the United States, United Kingdom, Germany, France, and Japan maintain full embassies in Ankara, while others operate consulates in Istanbul, Izmir, and Antalya.

Is there a website to locate embassies in Turkey?

Yes. You can locate embassies in Turkey through several online resources. The Turkish Ministry of Foreign Affairs website provides a directory of foreign embassies and consulates in the country. Additionally, many countries list their embassies and consulates abroad on their official government or foreign affairs websites. Websites like **embassy-worldwide.com** also provide a comprehensive, searchable list of embassies and consulates in Turkey. *For more details, see Chapter 16.*

Medical Facilities & Hospitals

Is there a number I can call for ambulance and fire emergencies?

In Turkey, you can call **112** for ambulance, fire, or police emergencies. It's the main number that will connect you quickly to the service you need.

If I am injured while on vacation in Turkey, are there hospitals that are recommended for tourists?

If you are injured while on vacation in Turkey, several hospitals cater well to international visitors. **Anadolu Medical Centre in Gebze, Acibadem Healthcare Group, Medipol University Hospital, Memorial Healthcare Group,** and **MedAmerican Polyclinic** in Istanbul are all highly recommended. These hospitals offer modern facilities, specialized care in areas like cardiology, oncology, and neurosurgery, and services for international patients, including English-speaking staff and assistance with appointments and accommodations. *For more details, see Chapter 17.*

Driving in Turkey

Which side of the road do I drive on?

In Turkey, you drive on the **right-hand side of the road.** Most vehicles have the steering wheel on the left, and traffic rules are similar to those in other European countries.

Can I use my driver's license from my home country to drive in Turkey?

Yes. You can use your valid foreign driver's license to drive in Turkey for a limited period, typically up to **six months**. It's recommended to also carry an **International Driving Permit** (**IDP**) alongside your original license, especially if it's not in Latin letters, to avoid any issues with local authorities or car rental companies.

How old do I need to be to rent a car?

In Turkey, you generally need to be at least **21 years old** to rent a car, though some rental companies may require drivers to be **23 or 25** depending on the vehicle type. Drivers under 25 are often charged a **young driver fee.** You also need a valid driver's license held for at least **one or two years**, depending on the rental company. *For more details, see Chapter 18.*

Nude Beaches & Clothing-Optional Resorts

Is public nudity legal on the beaches?

No. Public nudity is **not legal** on most beaches in Turkey. While some private or secluded beaches may tolerate topless sunbathing, full nudity is generally prohibited and can lead to fines or legal trouble. It's safest to follow local customs and wear standard swimwear. *For more details, see Chapter 19.*

Tourist Taxation

Is there room tax in Turkey?

Yes. Turkey charges a **tourist or accommodation tax** on hotel stays. It's usually a small amount per night, often a few Turkish Lira per person, and is either included in your bill or added separately at check-in or check-out. The exact rate can vary depending on the city and type of accommodation.

Is there any fee associated with leaving Turkey?

No. Turkey does **not charge a departure fee** for tourists leaving the country. Any airport fees are typically included in your airline ticket, so you don't need to pay extra at the airport when departing. *For more details, see Chapter 22.*

Long-Term Stays

Do I need to return to my home country to apply for a work permit in Turkey?

Not necessarily. You **do not always need to return to your home country** to apply for a work permit in Turkey. In many cases, you can apply while in Turkey on a valid residence or tourist visa, but the process usually involves your Turkish employer submitting an application on your behalf. Some nationalities may still need to start the process at a Turkish consulate abroad, so it's best to check the requirements specific to your country before applying.

As an American, how long can I stay in (country) without a visa?

As an American, you can stay in Turkey without a visa for **up to 90 days within a 180-day period** for tourism or business purposes. If you plan to stay longer or work, you will need to apply for the appropriate visa or residence permit. *For more details, see Chapter 23.*

In the Event of Death

What documents would an embassy need regarding the death of a tourist?

If a tourist dies in Turkey, the embassy generally requires several official documents to assist with repatriation or legal matters. These usually include the **death certificate** issued by the local Turkish authorities, a **passport** of the deceased, and any **identification documents.** The embassy may also request **medical reports or autopsy reports** if applicable, and a **consular registration** or notification form. In some cases, additional documents like a **power of attorney** from the family or **proof of relationship** for next of kin may be needed to handle arrangements. *For more details, see Chapter 25.*

EMERGENCY/IMPORTANT CONTACT NUMBERS IN TURKEY

Please consider putting some of these numbers in your phone **prior** to traveling to Turkey.

Emergency Numbers:

- 112 – Connects to ambulance, fire, and police

Specific Emergency Numbers

- **Police:** 155
- **Fire:** 110
- **Ambulance:** 112
- **Gendarmerie (rural law enforcement):** 156

Other Useful Contacts:

- **Tourist Police (Istanbul example):** 0 212 527 45 03
- **Coast Guard:** 158
- **Traffic Police / Roadside Assistance:** 154

- **Foreigners Communication Center (YIMER - visa/residence support):** 157

Legal Assistance:

Istanbul Bar Association

Phone: 0212 393 07 00
Website: www.istanbulbarosu.org.tr

Antalya Bar Association

Phone: 0242 238 61 55–59
Website: www.antalyabarosu.org.tr

İzmir Bar Association

Phone: +90 232 463 00 14
Email: info@izmirbarosu.org.tr
Website: www.izmirbarosu.org.tr

Union of Turkish Bar Associations

Phone: +90 312 292 59 00
Website: www.barobirlik.org.tr

USEFUL TURKISH PHRASES

Greetings

HI/HELLO – Merhaba (MEHR-ha-ba)

GOOD MORNING – Günaydın (GÜN-eye-dun)

GOOD AFTERNOON – Tünaydın / İyi günler (TÜN-eye-dun / EE-yee GÜN-ler)

GOOD NIGHT – İyi geceler (EE-yee GE-je-ler)

GOODBYE – Hoşça kal / Güle güle (HOSH-cha kahl / GÜ-leh GÜ-leh)

Magic Words

PLEASE – Lütfen (LOOT-fen)

THANK YOU – Teşekkür ederim (Teh-sheh-KOOR eh-deh-rim)

YOU'RE WELCOME – Rica ederim (REE-jah eh-deh-rim)

CHEERS! – Şerefe! (SHEH-reh-feh)

EXCUSE ME – Affedersiniz / Pardon (Af-fe-der-sin-iz / Par-don)

Getting Around

WHERE IS THE BATHROOM? – Tuvalet nerede? (Too-va-LET neh-REH-deh)

WHAT TIME IS IT? – Saat kaç? (Sa-AHT kach)

HOW DO I GET TO...? – ...'ya/'ye nasıl giderim? (...'ya/'ye NA-suhl GEE-deh-rim)

WHERE DOES THIS TRAIN/BUS GO? – Bu tren/otobüs nereye gidiyor? (Boo tren / oh-toh-BÜS neh-REH-yeh GEE-dee-yor)

RESTAURANT – Restoran (Res-toh-RAHN)

HOW MUCH DOES THIS COST? – Bu ne kadar? (Boo neh kah-DAR)

TRAIN/METRO STATION – Tren/metro istasyonu (Tren / MEH-tro ees-TAH-syo-noo)

Communication

DO YOU SPEAK ENGLISH? – İngilizce konuşuyor musunuz? (Een-gee-LEEZ-jeh koh-noo-SHOO-yor moo-soo-nooz)

I DO NOT UNDERSTAND – Anlamıyorum (Ahn-lah-MEE-yo-room)

I DON'T SPEAK TURKISH – Türkçe konuşamıyorum (TURK-cheh koh-noo-SHAH-muh-yo-room)

I DON'T KNOW – Bilmiyorum (BEEL-mee-yo-room)

Emergency

HELP! – Yardım edin! (YAR-dum eh-DIN)

CALL AN AMBULANCE! – Ambulans çağırın! (Ahm-BOO-lans cha-uh-RUHN)

I NEED A DOCTOR – Doktora ihtiyacım var (Dok-TOH-rah EEE-tee-ah-juh-m var)

POLICE – Polis (POH-lees)

I'M LOST – Kayboldum (KAI-bol-doom)

IT'S AN EMERGENCY – Acil bir durum (Ah-JEEL beer DOO-room)

GLOSSARY

ACQUITTAL: A jury verdict that a criminal defendant is not guilty, or the finding of a judge that the evidence cannot support a conviction.

ADVERSARY PROCEEDING: A lawsuit arising from a controversy that begins with filing a complaint.

AFFIDAVIT: A written statement made under oath.

APPEAL: A request made after a trial court has decided against one party in which the losing party asks a higher court to review the decision for legal error.

ARRAIGNMENT: A proceeding in which a criminal defendant is brought to court, told of the charges, and asked to plead guilty or not guilty.

BAIL: The temporary release of a person from jail when awaiting trial, on condition that a sum of money be lodged or deposited to guarantee an appearance in court.

BARRISTER: A lawyer admitted to plead at the Bar and who may try cases in superior court.

BURDEN OF PROOF: The duty to prove disputed facts.

CAUSE OF ACTION: A legal claim in a civil action.

COMPLAINT: A written statement that begins a civil lawsuit in which the plaintiff details the claims.

CONTRACT: An agreement between two or more persons to do something or to not do something.

CONVICTION: A judgment of guilt against a person charged with a crime.

CUSTOMS DUTY: A tariff or tax imposed on goods when transported across international borders.

COURT LIAISON: A person that coordinates with attorneys to perform administrative duties, such as scheduling witnesses, sharing information with law enforcement, and overseeing the reporting of cases to foreign embassies when applicable.

DAMAGES: Money that a defendant pays to a plaintiff in a civil case if the plaintiff wins.

DEFENDANT: 1) The individual against whom a civil claim is filed; 2) The individual against whom a criminal claim is filed.

FELONY: A serious crime, punishable by more than one year in prison.

MAGISTRATE: A judicial officer of a district court, who conducts initial proceedings in criminal cases, decides criminal misdemeanor cases, conducts many pretrial civil and criminal matters on behalf of district judges, and decides civil cases with the consent of the parties.

MISDEMEANOR: An offense punishable by one year or less in jail.

PLAINTIFF: A person or business that files a formal complaint with the court.

PLEA: In a criminal case, the answer of "guilty," "not guilty," or "no contest" in response to a criminal charge.

SOLICITOR: A lawyer who advises clients, represents them in lower court, and prepares cases for barristers to try in higher courts.

SOVEREIGN IMMUNITY: A legal doctrine by which the sovereign or the state (i.e. government) cannot commit a legal wrong and thus, it is immune from criminal and civil liability and cannot be sued.

STATUTE: A written law passed by a legislative body.

STATUTE OF LIMITATIONS: A statute prescribing a period of limitation to bring certain types of legal actions. If the action is not brought within that time, the person or entity (in a criminal context) is permanently barred from suing in court.

SUBPOENA: A command, issued under court authority, for a witness to appear and to give testimony.

TESTIMONY: Evidence presented orally by witnesses.

VERDICT: The decision of a judge or jury in a case.

WARRANT: Court authorization to conduct a search or to make an arrest.

ACKNOWLEDGMENTS

This book series would never have seen the light of day without the able assistance of the following people:

Kathy Adams, my paralegal for over 22 years, who is the "Best" I've ever worked with during my entire legal career because of her amazing work ethic, organizational skills, and her ability to think outside of the box in unique and creative ways;

Ally Knez-Siddique, a professional writer, and one of my paralegals, whose eye for detail, according to her, is both a blessing and a curse;

Gino Ibanez, my former law clerk, whose exceptional research skills helped move this book series along in its early stages;

Rosa Diaz Graham, my legal assistant who helped with research and word processing at the very beginning of this project;

Shelia Martin, one of my former paralegals, worked diligently on this series of books, even after taking on another job. Her organizational skills are reflected throughout;

Mindy Scarlett, my marketing and publishing "Guru"! Her creativity and vision have no boundaries!

ABOUT THE AUTHOR

Michael L. Moore practices in Orlando, Florida, the city where he spent his formative years. He credits the trauma of having his brother murdered when he was only 10 years old, as the catalyst that drew him into the practice of law.

Moore attended Florida State University, where he was a member of the FSU debate team. Upon graduating, he was awarded a full scholarship to attend the University of Tennessee College of Law, where he was elected President of the Student Bar Association. He further honed his advocacy and public speaking skills by participating in 'moot court' competitions.

After clerking at the Tennessee Attorney General's office while in law school, Moore moved back to Orlando, Florida, to work at the State Attorney's Office as a prosecutor, and where he was fortunate enough to meet the young lady that would eventually become his wife. Moore moved on to working for private law firms, both local and national, and eventually established his own law firm in 1999. He continues to make Orlando his home base.

It was the murder of a close friend and client in Jamaica that caused Moore to realize that books on laws in other countries were few and far between, and he was inspired to create Law of the Land Publishing. Moore launched Law of the Land Publishing to provide a series of guidebooks and a membership site for tourists and business travelers to stay up to date on the laws in each country they travel to, as well as having access to assistance if they run into legal issues.

"My vision is to educate people on what their legal rights are, and how they can access legal assistance, no matter where they have to travel to in the world," said Moore. "As Americans, we have a right to due process, but in some countries, you don't even have the right to access a square meal when incarcerated. My goal is to provide the information needed to stay out of trouble, as well as having access to assistance if trouble finds you."

www.ingramcontent.com/pod-product-compliance
Lightning Source LLC
Chambersburg PA
CBHW071435230926
51846CB00001B/245
* 9 7 8 1 9 6 4 8 7 0 2 3 6 *